Mother Teresa

A Symbol of Compassion

Mother Teresa

A Symbol of Compassion

J. Arivazagan

RAJ

RAJ PUBLICATIONS
New Delhi-110 002

Mother Teresa: A Symbol of Compassion

First Published in 2007

ISBN 13: 978-81-86208-56-4

ISBN 10: 81-86208-56-9

Published by : **Poonam Goel**
Raj Publications
108, 4855/24, Ansari Road
Daryaganj, New Delhi - 110 002

Tel.: 011 - 30120939

Laser Typesetting by : Tamalika Computers, Delhi

Printed at : Balaji Offset Printers, Delhi

PRINTED IN INDIA

To my mother,

Mrs. Thilagavathi,

who is my strength

in all my endeavours.

CONTENTS

Preface 9

1. Early Years 11
2. Loreto Convent 16
3. The 'Call' from God 21
4. Mother Teresa's Foundations 29
5. International Contribution 57
6. Awards and Recognition 73
7. Passing on the Crown 87
8. Beatification 101
9. A Symbol of Compassion 117

Appendix I. Quotes of Mother Teresa 124

II. Time Line 138

III. Lecture at U.S. Breakfast Prayer 141

IV. Homily of the Pope John Paul II 146

V. Prayers 154

Notes & References 159

PREFACE

Mother Teresa, the most famous and powerful woman of the twentieth century, is remembered globally as a person who treated members of various faiths as equal and served them with dedication and devotion. An Albanian-born Roman Catholic, Mother Teresa came to Calcutta in 1929 as a missionary to serve the famous Loreto Order. Eventually, she became the principal of St. Mary's School, a part of the Loreto Convent. Following the 'call' of God to serve Him in 'the unwanted, the unloved, the uncared for,' Mother Teresa left the Loreto Order in 1948 to serve the poor people of Calcutta. When she stepped out of the Loreto Convent to start her own Order of nuns, all she had was a five-rupee note and abundant faith in God.

In 1950, she founded the Missionaries of Charity. In addition to the three required vows of 'poverty, chastity and obedience', the Sisters of her Order took a fourth vow to render 'wholehearted and free service to the poorest of the poor. Through her Order, she established several homes for the dying destitute, abandoned children, leprosy afflicted and AIDS victims in India and several other countries. For nearly half a century, Mother Teresa served the poorest of the poor in Calcutta and across the globe, bringing them love and care.

Mother Teresa received many international awards for her work, including the Nobel Peace Prize and Bharat Ratna from the government of India. She cared little for the honors and attention heaped upon her by the world. In the face of hatred, rejection, loneliness and poverty, she continued to live and follow the guiding light of love that every religion, creed and denomination claims is the true face of God. During her lifetime itself, she was revered by many around the world as a 'living saint' for her work with the dispossessed. But she always considered herself as 'a pencil in the hands of God'.

Mother Teresa, who worked restlessly throughout her lifetime, died on 5 September 1997 and was finally rested in a plain-cemented grave with a small marble tombstone that bore her name and an apt epitaph: 'Love one another as I have loved you'. She will remain the world's most recognizable symbol of love and compassion forever.

In this book, I have attempted to put together the most significant part of Mother Teresa's life and her work.

I take this opportunity to thank my friends in Delhi, Mr. V. Raghunathan and Mrs. Shameemunisa, who first inspired me to work on this book, and Mr. K.M. Kumaran in Muscat, for his valuable support and encouragement.

This book would not have taken the present shape had the publisher, Mr. Pawan Goyal, not given me sufficient time to complete. I sincerely thank his patience and understanding.

1

Early Years

Mother Teresa was born on 26 August 1910 in a Catholic Albanian family in Skopje, capital of the vilayet of Kosova in Northern Macedonia, then part of the Ottoman Empire, just north of Greece. She was the third child to Nicholas Bojaxhiu and Dranafile Bernai. She was christened Agnes-Gonxha Bojaxhiu on August 27, 1910. She had an elder sister Age, born in 1904 and elder brother Lazar, born in 1907. Nicholas Bojaxhiu was a well-known building contractor and wholesale food importer in Skopje. He was a member of the Skopje town council and built the first Skopje Theatre.

Nicholas was known as a generous local benefactor and encouraged his children to be generous and compassionate to those less fortunate than themselves. He traveled frequently in the region and kept in touch with political realities. When the Yugoslavs and Albanians were fighting for Kosova and other provinces of Albania in which was the city of Skopje, Nicholas was involved in active politics and tried to obtain the national rights for Albanians. He was in close contact with several of the Nationalist leaders, and politics was frequently discussed at home.

Agnes's mother, Dranafile, was obviously the more religious of the parents. She took the children to the church for morning mass most days and when not working in the house or helping others, she was always saying the rosary. She never turned away those in need who reached her door, whether seeking food, shelter, clothing or even money. As a child, Agnes was 'plump, round and tidy' soon acquired the nickname 'Gonxha', meaning 'flower bud'. She was known by her nickname in Albania. Agnes who grew up into a studious, book-loving girl, always accompanied her mother to deliver parcels of food and money to the poor.

Agnes, Lazar and Age attended their early education at an elementary school within the Sacred Heart Church, where the lessons were in taught in Serbo-Croat language. Later the children attended state schools, Gymnasia. The home they lived in was a large one with a pleasant garden and flowers and fruit trees, on the same street as the Church of the Sacred Heart. The Bojaxhiu family had a comfortable and prosperous childhood, which was suddenly brought to an end.

In 1917, Nicholas travelled 160 miles to Belgrade to attend a political meet. Some days later, he staggered to his home and in a few hours he died under mysterious circumstances. Some accounts say that his support for a

Greater Albania would have earned him many enemies and he would have probably been poisoned when he attended a political dinner at Belgrade.

The lives of the Bojaxhiu children changed dramatically after their father's death. Nicholas's business partners misappropriated the firms' assets, leaving the widow and her children with just the roof over their heads. Dranafile struggled to rear her three children for a short while. Then, she started a small business of her own that of selling embroidered cloth, turning adversity into enterprise and brought up the three children with her earnings. The family frequented the Sacred Heart Church more than before and Agnes along with her sister started involving in parish activities. She was a soprano, while her sister was a contralto, not just in the local church choir, but in the Albanian Catholic choir too. The two sisters performed at charity concerts that took place almost every month, usually organized by the young Catholics. The family gathered in the living room every evening to say the rosary. Agnes was influenced by her mother 's deep faith in God, her love for neighbours and her charitableness even at a time of adversity. Agnes started moving in a religious direction.

When Agnes was 12 years old, she felt the desire to become a nun. When she told her mother, she was opposed, as she was a child then. In due course, Agnes forgot her first impulse. She spent many hours in prayers at church and late in her home. She joined a branch of a society called Sodality of the Blessed Virgin Mary, started by Father Franjo

Jambrenkovic, a Jesuit Priest, who later became the Pastor of the Scared Heart in 1925.

In the Sodality, Agnes learnt about the lives of saints and missionaries. Father Jambrenkovic taught the girls about the Yugolsav Jesuits who went on a mission to the province of Bengal in India in 1924. Their experiences with the people, especially the children in India, were recounted to the members of the Sodality. All these descriptions about the missionary work deeply influenced young Agnes and she became interested in the world of missionaries.

At the age of 18, Agnes received her first 'call' to a vocation as a missionary nun. She felt that God wanted her to join the spiritual life and belong completely to Him. She decided to leave her family and loved ones to become a missionary to India. She also learnt that there was an Irish order, the Loreto Sisters, serving in Bengal whose main work was in the field of education. She turned to Father Jambrenkovic to ascertain whether the 'Call' she had received was genuine. He explained to her that 'Call of God had necessarily to be accompanied by a feeling of deep joy, especially where this was an indication of life's vocation.' Agnes decided that her vocation was to be a missionary to India. and she had no doubt of her decision in choosing a life of self-sacrifice, which she strongly felt was God's choice.

When Agnes conveyed her decision of becoming a missionary to India to her mother, she went to her room, closed the door and did not re-emerge for twenty-four hours. She was quite upset about her daughter's decision because, in those days, the missionaries never returned to their homes. However, realizing that it was God's will, she came out and advised her young daughter, 'Put your hand in His hand and walk all the way with Him'.

Meanwhile, Lazar, who had joined the Albania's Military Academy after his studies, on September 1, 1928, joined the new monarchy of King Zog I, Albania as second Lieutenant in the army.

Agnes was informed that she had to serve the Loreto Abbey in Rathfarman in Ireland and learn some English prior to serving the Loreto Order in Bengal. On 26 September 1928, Agnes accompanied by her mother and sister, left Skopje for Zagreb by train. The members of the Sodality, friends and relatives bade a tearful farewell to Agnes. She spent a few days with her mother and sister in Zagreb. When finally she waved her goodbye at the Zagreb station, Agnes and her mother knew that they would never meet again.

Agnes spent two months as a young postulant at the Loreto Abbey in Rathfarman near Dublin and learnt English. In November 1928, she set sail for India to enter into a new world of sacrifice and service, which had been her dream and true goal.

2

Loreto Convent

Agnes reached Bombay and from there she traveled to Calcutta by train. On 6 January 1926, she reached Calcutta and spent a few days. On 16 January 1929, she was sent to the Loreto Novitiate in Darjeeling to begin her novitiate, the customary period of spiritual development to determine suitability for a ruled life of obedience, fidelity and faith. She stayed at the Loreto Convent, one of the several schools run by missionaries, where mainly British children as well as a few from wealthy Indian children studied.

In May 1929, she received the 'holy habit' (the religious dress of Loreto). She wore the black habit and a veil as a Loreto nun. As a novice, Agnes was given a thorough grounding in the habits of prayer and the works of the apostolate. Like other novices, Agnes taught poor children two hours a day, as on the job training, as it were. She concentrated more on English lessons from the very beginning and picked up a little Hindi and Bengali as well.

The daily activities in the Convent kept Agnes totally absorbed and two years went by quickly for her.

On 24 May 1931, as a nun of Loreto Convent, Agnes took her first vows, those of 'poverty, chastity and obedience' She was inspired to take her name in religious life from St. Theresa of Lisieux. Later, this was referred to the first sign of the contemplative side of her mission for taking St. Theresa of Lisieux as a saintly guide. Theresa, the youngest child of a French watchmaker and his wife, was 15 years old when she joined the Carmelite Order of sisters at in 1888. She informally made a vow, and formally on two occasions as a professed Carmelite nun, to 'refuse nothing to Jesus'. She announced that her vocation was 'love' and that one of her principles was to pray for priests and missionaries. She longed to be sent forth in the missions as a herald of God's love. Since her frailty prevented this, she rejoiced in being assigned missionaries for whom she prayed and regarded with great affection as her spiritual brothers. Her 'little way' was 'the way of spiritual childhood, the way of trust and absolute self surrender'. She considered herself as 'a ball in the hands of the Child Jesus'. She died of tuberculosis in 1897 at the early age of twenty-four. In 1927, twenty-five years after her death, the Vatican canonized her with the title St. Theresa of Lisieux.

Agnes's choice of 'Theresa' as her professed name indicated her fervour for not just becoming a religious, but wanting clearly to do missionary work – 'to go out and give the life of Christ to the people'. Sister Breen, who had completed her novitiate the year before, had already taken the name of 'Theresa' from St. Theresa of Avila. To avoid confusion, Agnes decided to spell in the Spanish way, 'Teresa'.

After she completed her novitiate, Sister Teresa, as she was now called, was sent to teach at St. Mary's School, a part of Loreto Convent in the Calcutta suburb of Entally. At St. Mary's school, most of the boarders were orphans or children whose parents were unable to look after them. For the next few years, Sister Teresa taught geography, history and catechism, and performed several other duties. She also helped Mother Du Cenacle who was the principal at St. Mary's. In addition to her teaching duties, she was given charge of the Daughters of St. Anne, a diocesan congregation founded by Loreto. This branch conducted school in the Bengali medium and the Daughters wore saris instead of the European habit. She was referred to as "Bengali Teresa" to distinguish her from Sister Theresa (Breen).

On 24 May 1937, Sister Teresa took her final vows. . From that very day, she was renamed as 'Mother Teresa'. Between 1936 and 1937, Mother Teresa supervised St. Teresa's Primary school, 'Bengali Medium' at Lower Circular Road. There, she organized classes for primary school children. She taught catechism well with many examples from her own life and would make the subject 'come alive'.

Mother Teresa and other members of the Sodality of Mary visited the slum dwellers of Motijhil, which was situated on the other side of the wall of the Entally compound, and which later became her first venture.

When the Second World War got intensified due to occupation of Burma by Japan, Calcutta became the operational center. There were occasional air raids on Calcutta. Military authorities evacuated many buildings. The normal life at the Loreto Convent was disrupted by the turbulent events. In 1942, the Loreto complex at Entally was converted into a makeshift military hospital, and St. Mary's school was shifted to a building on Convent Road.

Between 1942 and 1943, the Great Bengal Famine stalked the land and people were starving on the roads. As a trained nurse, Sister Teresa nursed the famine-ridden and sick during the war. She knew the poverty of Calcutta and its people and wanted to work for them, but only through the Convent as a Loreto nun. Father Henry, a Belgian priest, who taught catechism at St. Mary's, influenced Mother Teresa to work in the slums.

In 1944, Mother Teresa became the Principal at St. Mary's. On July 12, 1944, Mother Teresa met Father Celeste Van Exem in Baitha-kana, Calcutta, for the first time. Father van Exem, a member of the Society of Jesus, came to Calcutta from his native Belgium during the Second World War. He had earlier spent several years in the Middle East and spoke fluent Arabic. During the war he was asked to perform Mass at St. Mary's School in its temporary abode in the Convent Street. He became her closest friend, spiritual director and father of her spiritual journey.

Mother Teresa was thoroughly happy at the St. Mary's school, first as a teacher and then as the Principal. Mother, not ordinarily a physically strong woman, succumbed to tuberculosis. She was unable to continue teaching and was sent to Darjeeling, in the foothills of the Himalayas for treatment as well as to make her retreat. And that was the beginning of her voyage of selfless service and sacrifice.

3

THE 'CALL' FROM GOD

In 1946, India was on the verge of freedom from British rule. These were days of great turmoil and unrest in India. The Muslim League was clamoring for an independent country of Pakistan to be carved out of the west and east wings of undivided India. Mohamed Ali Jinnah, leader of the Muslim League had just called for and successfully executed "Direct Action Day" [started on August 16th, 1946]. With Jinnah's approval, the Moslems started violent action and riots against their Hindu neighbours and the civilian authorities to prove that Indians of different religions could not live together peacefully. These beliefs and actions contradicted what Mahatma Gandhi and the Congress Party were teaching. Rioting and bloodshed continued until the Congress Party gave in to hand over Pakistan to Mohammed Ali Jinnah. It was if they had determined that it was better to have emergency surgery to remove the affected parts and thus save the main body of India. It was on one of those hectic days that Mother Teresa received the call from God to serve the poor.

On 10 September 1946, in a train to Darjeeling to make her retreat, Mother Teresa heard the 'Call' – the call from God to serve Him in the poor. The Call continued in Darjleeing throughout her retreat. 'The message was quite clear, it was an order. I was to leave the Convent. I felt God wanted something more from me. He wanted me to be poor and to love Him in the distressing disguise of the poorest of the poor', she explained later. Mother Teresa had often explained this as a 'Call within a Call'. She would remain as nun but the work would change – to serve the poorest of the poor outside the convent.

In October 1946, when Mother Teresa returned from Darjeeling she met Father van Exem and showed him the small slips of paper where she had written down the Inspiration and asked for his views and guidance as she wanted to leave Loreto convent. She explained to him that it was the Will of God. Father Van Exem was very impressed and felt that she had a real 'Call'. He told her to wait for three-four months before the matter could be raised with Archbishop Perier. Mother Teresa was a happy Loreto nun and her teaching in the convent school was immensely rewarding, yet, she decided to sacrifice it. She later admitted that leaving Loreto convent was a greater sacrifice than leaving her family and country to enter religious life.

Though Mother Teresa had decided to go to serve the poor in the streets, it was not easy for her to leave Loreto

Convent. It required several complex permissions and had to undergo a lengthy process. She had to obtain permission to be released from Loreto Order. She also needed the permission of Vatican to work directly with the poor, not as a laywoman but as a vowed nun, by the indent of Exclaustration (meaning – allowing her to leave the Convent and remain as a religious nun, committed to her vows and under the obedience of Archbishop). Mother Teresa, as always, prayed and had abundant faith that everything would come through.

In January 1947, Mother Teresa wrote to Archbishop Perier about the 'Will of God'. Father Van Exem personally handed over the letter to Archbishop Perier. Initially, the Archbishop refused. He felt that it would not be safe for a lone European nun to be on the streets of Calcutta, at a time when political and communal riots were going on. However, he advised her to wait for a year and strictly told her that her intention should remain secret.

Meanwhile, Mother Teresa was transferred to Asansol, a city about 175 miles north-west of Calcutta. Mother Teresa had to wait the whole year of Indian Independence. At the end of 1947, Archbishop Perier finally permitted Mother Teresa to write to Mother Gertrude M. Kennedy, the Mother General of Loreto at Rathfarman, asking for permission to be released from the Loreto Order. On February 2, 1948, she received Mother General's letter permitting her to send an application, directly to Rome. In the letter, Mother Teresa explained her call and sought permission to work in the slums as a nun, by an Indent of Exclaustration. Days passed by, Mother Teresa waited for the reply. Finally at the end of July 1948, Archbishop Perier conveyed to Father van Exem that Mother Teresa had been granted the Indent of Exclaustration, with a caution that she should remain outside cloister for one year, at the end of which Archbishop Perier had been authorized to decide whether she should continue her work or return to Loreto. When Father van Exem revealed about the reply from Archbishop and gave her the Vatican decree, Mother Teresa's very first question was, 'Father can I go the slums now"?

The message that Mother Teresa was granted permission to leave Loreto Convent spread like wildfire not only in Entally but also among the Catholic missionaries in Calcutta. It came as shocking news to many of the Loreto nuns as Mother Teresa had never discussed with them. Letters went out to every Loreto institution in India to pray for her vocation. Mother Teresa informed her mother in Skopje that she was leaving the Loreto Order with the permission of the Vatican and with her religious vows intact.

On the evening of 16 August 1948, Mother Teresa removed her old religious habit and wore a new habit. Her new dress consisted of a simple cotton white sari with blue borders (blue was the color of Virgin Mary), as those of the sweepers of Calcutta, which became her trademark religious dress. Mother Teresa asked Father van Exem to bless the three white saris, a small cross and a rosary. As her she wish was to work in the slums, Father Van Exem advised her to take some medical training, which was essential, to which Mother Teresa readily agreed to undergo. She left the Convent at Entally on 17 August 1948 and proceeded to Patna for medical training.

In Patna, she took training in nursing, dispensary and hospital work at the American Medical Missionaries. Some accounts say that Mother Teresa had the first experience of suffering of the poor Indians during her training in this hospital. Once a man came to Mother Teresa carrying a bundle. She saw that two dry twigs were hanging out of the bundle. On close inspection, she was shocked to find that they were not twigs, but abnormally thin legs of a completely blind child who was on the verge of death. The man was afraid that she might refuse to accept the child. He told her that if she did not want the child, he would throw the child into the grass. Hearing that, her heart froze. She took the child into her arms. The child had found a second mother.

In 1948, after spending almost four months in Patna, Mother Teresa returned to Calcutta in December. At that time Calcutta had a harrowing vision: stratified, class conscious, and also abysmally poor. She stayed at St. Joseph's Home, which was run by the Little Sisters for the Poor.

In the end of December 1948, she stepped out of the security of the cloister and started her work in Motijhil, a slum nearby the Loreto Convent. She had no money or companion or helper when she left the convent. All that she had was abundant faith that God would guide and protect her in her way ahead. Some even remarked that she had entered into an uncertain future. But she remained undeterred and continued her work.

Mother Teresa visited families in the slums, washed the sores of some children, cared for an old man lying sick on the road and nursed a woman dying of hunger and TB. She started each day in communion with Jesus in the Eucharist and then went out, rosary in her hand, to find and serve Him in "the unwanted, the unloved, the uncared for." She started her first school for the slum children in Motijil, which was an open spot under a tree. There were no desks, blackboard or chalks. She approached the families of the children who attended St. Mary's parish school and appealed to them to send their children to her new school. She went to meet the parish priest of Park Circus who gave her 100 rupees to show his appreciation for her work. She immediately rented two new rooms in front of a big tank, to be used for school and dispensary. Within a fortnight, Mother Teresa opened both a school and a dispensary. Subsequently, she opened her second school in Tiljala in January 1949. In the meanwhile, within a few weeks after she had started her work in Motijhil, people began to express doubts about her activities. Even her students at Loreto Convent were suspicious of her motives in helping street children and orphans. These rumblings reached the ears of Mother Provincial in Entally who desired Mother Teresa's to return to Loreto. But with her determination and faith in God, she continued her work in the slums serving the poorest of the poor.

St. Joseph's Home, where Mother Teresa had been staying, was far away from the Motijil Slum. Father Van Exem realized that Mother Teresa should stay in a more convenient place closer to the slum where she worked. He started to find a suitable place for her and found one at 14, Creek Lane - owned by two brothers, Michael and Alfred Gomes. On 28 February 1949, Mother Teresa moved into an empty room on the top floor of the Gomes' residence. There was no furniture in the room. Michael Gomes offered some furniture but she was reluctant to use them . However, she accepted some packaging cases and these served as seats as well as chairs.

After three weeks Mother Teresa had moved into Creek Lane, she had a small band of followers, including some of her former students at St. Mary's school. On March 19, 1949, Subashini Das, a pupil of Mother Teresa joined as her first postulant. Subashini Das later took the holy name Sister Agnes. On April 26, another former student at St. Mary's school, Magdalena Gomes, became the second postulant and took the name Sister Gertrude. In the next few months many young women came to join Mother Teresa, most of them had been her former students. She warned young women who wanted to join her that it was a work only few persons could endure and told each volunteer that only a 'burning fire' would succeed.

Soon, these Sisters dressed in distinctive white saris with blue bands, became a familiar sight not only in Creek Lane but also in Motijhil and other slums where they served the poor. They ran school in the mornings and the dispensary in the evenings. Mother Teresa with her Sisters begged from door to door and passed the things they got from begging, to the people who were starving on the streets. Sometimes, her landlord, Michael Gomes also accompanied her in the begging expedition. The Sisters took great care of the sick and the dying and taught the children about the dignity of human life. Their great faith and unselfish love for others helped Mother Teresa and her sisters do the most menial tasks joyfully. Mother taught her nuns to serve everyone as if he or she were Jesus, and to work with joy and happiness in their hearts. Mother Teresa herself set the pace by declaring "the poor deserve not only service and dedication but also the joy that belongs to human love"

4

MOTHER TERESA'S FOUNDATIONS

Mother Teresa and her Sisters continued to serve the slums from the small place at Creek Lane and her new Order of nuns was not recognized as a separate congregation till the end of 1949. By the beginning of 1950, the Archbishop Perier approved their way and Father van Exem was given the task of writing the Constitution for the new Congregation, which is presently called 'The Constitutions of the Missionaries of Charity'. The Vatican originally labeled Mother Teresa's new Congregation as the 'Diocesan Congregation of the Calcutta Diocese,' but later came to be known as the 'Missionaries of Charity'. Mother Teresa had explained the mission of her new Congregation was "to care for the hungry, the naked, the homeless, the crippled, the blind, the lepers, all those people who feel unwanted, unloved, uncared for throughout society, people that have become a burden to the society and are shunned by everyone. Accordingly to Navin Chawla, "if one had to choose two words to sum up Mother Teresa's underlying concept of the congregation, then these might very easily be the words 'I thirst'. These words represent Christ's symbolic cry of spiritual love and acceptance. They also serve as a ...for each Missionary of Charity of the general aim of the Society, which is to quench the infinite thirst of Jesus on the Cross by a life of Prayer, contemplation and penance. As a means to better understand the special call 'to love and serve Christ in the distressing disguise of the poor', the Missionaries of Charity are prepared to accept suffering, renunciation and even death."

Normally, the members of Catholic religious orders take the three required vows of 'chastity, poverty and obedience.' Unique to her congregation, Mother Teresa added the fourth vow: "wholehearted and free service to the poorest of the poor." The Sisters refer to this fourth vow as 'our way'. On 7 October 1950, the Constitutions were approved by the Sacred Congregation in Rome. The Order's guiding theme was her own: "Let every action of mine be something beautiful for God." In the same year Mother Teresa took up Indian citizenship.

After the partition of India, Calcutta became a city with great human misery. Three million people were without home, jobs and slept on pavements. There was a dangerous rise in the number of refugees, destitute and sick people. People were dying on the street as hospitals ran out of spaces to accommodate them.

During this period, Mother Teresa was once traveling in a tram on the way to her 'begging expedition' along with

Michael Gomes to get some medicines. She saw a dying man on the roadside under a tree. She decided to give the man some shelter on her way back. After collecting the medicines she rushed to the spot only to find the man dead. This incident had a deep impact on Mother Teresa and she decided to find a place for the dying and destitute, where they could have a dignified death.

NIRMAL HRIDAY

Mother Teresa and her Sisters picked up the poor and dying people from the pavements and took them to the hospitals. Sometimes, the hospitals could not accommodate them due to lack of beds. When Mother Teresa found hospitals refusing to take in destitute who were left to die on the streets, she decided to start a home for them. She first used her small dispensary in the Motijhil slum, which hardly had any space to administer more than two patients.

Mother Teresa approached the Chief Medical Officer of the Calcutta Municipality and asked him to provide her space for her venture. Recognising the public value of the work she had been doing, he showed her two large halls adjoining to the city's famous temple Kalighat. On 22 February 1952, Mother Teresa opened the Kalighat Home for the Dying, which she named Nirmal Hriday (meaning Pure Heart). People dying off the streets of Calcutta were brought here and taken care of.

In an interview with Malcolm Muggeridge, the author of the book 'Something Beautiful for God', Mother Teresa told how she for the first time had picked up a dying woman from the street. 'The woman was half eaten up by rats and ants. I took her to the hospital, but they could do nothing for her. They only took her because I refused to go home unless something was done for her. After they cared for her, I went straight to the townhall and asked for a place where I could take these people, because that day I found more people dying in the street. The employee of health services brought me to the temple of Kali and showed me the 'dormashalah' where the pilgrims used to rest after they worshipped the goddess Kali. The building was empty and he asked me if I wanted it. I was very glad with the offer for many reasons, but especially because it was the center of prayer for Hindus. Within 24 hours we brought our sick and suffering and started the Home for the Dying Desitutes.'

When Nirmal Hriday was opened, not everyone in the locality liked the idea of a place for dying near the temple. The temple priests even asked city authorities to relocate the newly named Nirmal Hriday. A group of locals protested and even hurled stones at the Sisters. Once, a man threatened her that he would kill her and her immediate response was that if he killed her, she would hope to reach God sooner. One day a leader of a group of young people entered Nirmal Hriday with an intention to throw the Sisters out. But on entering the room, he saw the Sisters treating the abnormal bodies of sick people with love and care. He soon left the room and told the group that he would throw the Sisters out only on one condition that they should request their mothers and Sisters to start the same kind of service to the poor like Mother Teresa.

Another strange incident diminished the antagonism of the temple priests and local people. A young temple priest who was found in the advanced stage of tuberculosis was refused admission in the hospitals and even his family had let him down to die. He was brought to Nirmal Hriday where Mother Teresa personally nursed him. When he died, she sent his body to be cremated as per Hindu rites, an act which finally won the admiration of most of the Hindus.

There were many religious and social organizations of all sizes and denominations in and around Calcutta that provided succour to the poor and ailing. Yet none actually took in those destitutes who could find neither home nor hospital to die in. For the Hindu mind, unshakeable in its belief in the transmigration of souls, the ailing body is beside the point. It is merely to be cast off to free the soul to continue its cycle of birth, death and rebirth in its pursuit of salvation. Mother Teresa and her Missionary Sisters, however, felt that it was important to touch the broken bodies and unattended souls with their compassion. Yet one would entirely miss the point if one failed to grasp that, for them, each occupant of the stretcher beds in Nirmal Hriday is the sick, abandoned or dying Christ. Without this unshakeable conviction, they would be as unable to do this work as anyone else. It is this that is fundamental to the philosophy of the Missionaries of Charity, not the conversion of souls nor giving the bodies a Christian burial, which, unless especially indicated or requested, would be considered by Mother Teresa to be a sacrilege.

At Nirmal Hriday, when the poor are brought at the hospice, filthy and eaten by vermin and disease, they are washed, their hair cut and their wounds dressed. They are fed and taken care. The sisters help them get better, or at least try to give them a measure of peace before death. And almost half of the people do die; their bodies are cremated according to the religion they belong to.

Beyond the food, shelter, clothing and medication, the ultimate gifts that Mother Teresa gave to the poor were love and compassion. She reached the wounded heart and broken spirit. She transformed pain and suffering into love and healing. Mother once said of Nirmal Hriday, "You feel the presence of God there, and they [the poor] feel the love they get. Like one of them said, `I've lived like an animal in the street but I will die like an angel,' with love and care."

Work at Nirmal Hriday is tough and as unending as the vicissitudes of suffering there. Once a month the patients are moved and the furniture aired so that the ward, cleaned daily, can be scrubbed down floor to ceiling.

Volunteers come for short periods. It is the Sisters who are the backbone of Kalighat. Theirs is an incredibly difficult service. To being with, it is necessary to be physically strong, as the work involves being nurse, porter and doctor rolled into one, often working eighteen hours at a time, six days a week. It is an endless succession of medication, washing, feeding and cleaning, or simply sitting by to listen to a request, a prayer or a complaint. To sheer physical strength, add compassion and a sense of humour. 'He got a ticket straight to St. Peter', or 'She went smilings, she died such a beautiful death,' is a frequent refrain. Despite it being difficult work, all the Missionaries of Charity must be prepared to work with the dying. The irony is that most of them actually plead to be sent to Kalighat. Since this is simply not possible, most must make do with short stings before being sent elsewhere.

In the wards of Nirmal Hriday lie the emaciated, skin-and-bone inmates. They are the desperately poor, victims of malnourishment and illness, those who inhabit the crevices of the big city of Calcutta. Nirmal Hriday has offered them a place of repose, where they can get free basic medical attention, often for festering body sores and gangrene, or for infectious diseases like tuberculosis; where they are given nutritious food; where they, unimaginably, are the guests of honour, caringly ministered to.

Pope John Paul II, during his Apostolic Pilgrimage to India in February 1986, visited Nirmal Hriday in Calcutta. In his address, he said:

'Nirmal Hriday is a place of suffering, a house familiar with anguish and pain, a home for the destitute and dying. But, at the same time, Nirmal Hriday is a place of hope, a house built on courage and faith, a home where love reigns, a home filled with love.

In Nirmal Hriday, the mystery of human suffering meets the mystery of faith and love. And in this meeting, the deepest questions of human existence make themselves heard. The pain-filled body and spirit cries out: "Why? What is the purpose of suffering? Why must I die?" And the answer that comes, often in unspoken ways of kindness and compassion, is filled with honesty and faith: " I cannot fully answer all your questions; I cannot take away all your pain. But of this I am sure: God loves you with an everlasting love. You are precious in his sight. In him I love you too. For in God we are truly brothers and sisters".

Nirmal Hriday proclaims the profound dignity of every human person. The loving care which is shown here bears witness to the truth that the worth of a human being is not measured by usefulness or talents, by health or sickness, by age or creed or race. Our human dignity comes from God our Creators in whose image we are all made. No amount of privation or suffering can ever remove this dignity, for we are always precious in the eyes of God.

The Apostle Saint John tells us: "Our love is not to be just words or mere talk, but something real and active" May these words of Saint John be true for each one of us May the courageous love and living faith which we find here at Nirmal Hriday inspire in us the same real and active love.'

Since the founding of Nirmal Hriday, the Sisters picked up thousands of men, women and children from the streets of Caluctta and brought them to Nirmal Hriday and gave them a dignified life before their death.

In February 2006, Mr. Pawel, a traveler visited Calcutta with one thing in his mind – to volunteer at Mother Teresa's Nirmal Hriday. He gave an interesting account of what he had been doing at the Home:

"Day One: I enter Nirmal Hriday with little apprehension. How bad will it be? The surroundings are already unsettling. The home is next to the Kali Temple - the worship place of a Hindu goddess who requires ritualistic daily sacrifice of tens of animals (mostly goats). As I enter Nirmal Hriday (Pure Heart), I see a big room with 50 beds. On them are dying people, or rather, live human skeletons. If you've ever seen footage of famine in Ethiopia or the pictures of the liberation of Auschwitz, you get the feeling. They all lie in three rows - all men, too weak to move, many with limbs eaten away by leprosy or disfigured by some other disease. It feels like a run-down hospital ward during the Great Depression era. On the other side of the building, there is a similar scene with 50 women. A few nuns, in their instantly recognizable blue-rimmed white saris, supervise 20 or so volunteers. In between the patient rooms, there is a large, dark laundry/kitchen room. As I enter, ten volunteers are doing laundry, the Indian way. In huge, stone basins, they jump on piles of soaked clothes and blankets. Others are busy rinsing clothes. The water is sloshing all around. Everybody is barefoot. The air smells of hospital disinfectant. The contrast between the energetic washing and the stillness of the dying patients across the wall is stark. An Italian friend later described the scene as purely Dante-esque, but I yet have to read Dante to confirm it.

Initially, I am reluctant to go straight to the patient room. I want to adjust to the scenery. Luckily, I get assigned the wringing of the clothes. This goes on for a while and my hands start to hurt. When I'm almost done, a dead body - all wrapped up in white linen - is carried out of the small room in the back and through the laundry room. The body is adorned in flowers. Everybody stops for a minute. One of the seasoned volunteers puts more flowers on the body, and soon the body disappears and we continue our washing. I am struck by how little sorrow everybody has shown. I will understand why later on.

I catch a glimpse of a man lying down in the corner of the room. I see one of the nuns sitting on the bedside, just touching the dying man's head. There is nothing but pure love on her face. Her hands are so gentle, so comforting - this is exactly what I came here for, to experience something like this, nothing but pure love. I sit next to her. The man's name is Oujia. Somebody found him on the streets. The nun says that his family most likely rejected him, not able to care for him - this is the case with most patients at Nirmal Hriday. He is dying, unconscious, breathing slowly and heavily. He is the epitome of human suffering. His skin is all wrinkled and dehydrated, cheekbones sunken deep, and his fingernails are black with dirt. The whole body is ravaged by malnutrition. I am deeply moved. The nun leaves me alone with him. I try to think like Mother Teresa, who said that every one of these patients is Jesus in disguise. But it is not necessary for me to create that religious image. In fact, I immediately see Oujia as simply somebody close to me, a family member. It could have been my brother, or my father, or my son. I don't know why, but I start referring to him as my son. I am overcome by sorrow. There is no need that anybody should die like this.After a while, the sorrow gives way to compassion, or rather simply pure love. I sit there holding his hand for a long time. It's OK. You are going home. Just a little bit longer. The feeling is peaceful and uplifting. There are no other emotions, just this one. It's rare that I get to experience it. Sometimes when I visit my son in California, I get that feeling, but most often there is so much else going on that it is hard to stop and simply feel. This is the joy of Nirmal Hriday - there is nothing else to really feel. All you have to do is hold somebody's hand and simply be there. It's revealing when you think that among the dying, you can experience the best part of life.

Day 2: I come in the afternoon. There are too many volunteers in the morning and not enough in the afternoon. From now on, I will come only in the afternoon. Things are quieter. There is no laundry to do. I spend a lot of time with Oujia. A Japanese journalist comes to photograph the place. When she sees Oujia, she is deeply moved. She stands silent for a while, then she just kneels down next to him, takes his hand, and starts sobbing.

Day 3: As soon as I enter, I see Oujia's bed empty. He died earlier during the day. I wish I was there. I see his body in the little room in the back, already wrapped in white, waiting for cremation. The inscription on the wall says, "I am on my way to heaven." I say my last goodbyes, but can't spend too much time. With fewer volunteers, there are things to do - food to serve, urine, and stool to wipe, clothes to change, arthritic legs to massage.

Day 4: Things become more routine. I start to get the rhythm of the place. I know which patients can go to the bathroom and which wet themselves and need wiping and changing. A few need to exercise - you hold them by their arms and try to get them to walk. Their legs are so weak that it is more like dragging them through the room than walking. I try to not get lost in the "doing". It is not always as easy as it was with Oujia. Many patients are mentally ill. Some scream at you with frustration for not understanding Bengali. Some just scream. There is this one patient who loves to count to 100 in English and to give massages to the volunteers. He is cheerful; I often sit next to him. He starts gently punching on my arms and legs, counting with every punch: one, two, three, four.... Sometimes he stops his counting, and starts talking to the crucifix on the wall, pointing to me and to the crucifix as if he was really having a conversation. It's eerie. I wish I understood Bengali. Four people die today.

Day 5: As I get more and more accustomed with the place, I get to talk to the nuns a little more. They have such devotion for their patients. Could I do this for the rest of my life? I don't know. I haven't spent enough time there to ponder this question. I have only one more day to volunteer, and so I won't get the answer, but it's OK. I found my joy in this city, even if for just a few days.

Mr. Pawel concluded: 'There are no photographs in this entry. If you really want to see how it looks, you probably can find some on the internet. I did not want to be a photographer there. Besides, it is easy to photograph hunger, death, and disease. Nirmal Hriday for me is not about any of these. It's about love, and that is much harder to capture on camera.'"

MOTHER HOUSE

In two years since the recognization of her order in 1950, about thirty young women joined the Order and the top floor of 14 Creek Lane was entirely occupied. They needed to move to a larger place. Mother Teresa began to search for a house.

In 1953, Mother Teresa located a property in Lower Circular Road, which belonged to a Magistrate. She bought the property with the help of an interest-free loan advanced by the Church. In February, the Minssionaries of Charity Sisters moved into the building at 54A Lower Circular Road (now Acharya Jagdish Chandra Bose Road). This home came to be known as Mother House and served as the Head Quarters of Missionaries of Charity.

CO-WORKERS

In 1954, the group called the Co-Workers of Mother Teresa was founded by Ann Blaikie, a British lawyer. The group members are individuals from all faiths (and non-faiths) and walks of life. They are just ordinary people who believe that everyone deserves the chance to be loved and cared for. Originally, the group volunteered to buy clothing for the children of Calcutta for their religious holidays. The Co-Workers then began also to buy medicine and other needed supplies for the Missionaries of Charity. Since 1954, the group membership has expanded to more than 3 million individuals in more than 70 countries.

SHISHU BHAVAN

In 1956, Mother Teresa opened the Shishu Bhavan close to Motherhouse for the children. It was a two story dwelling located a few blocks away from the Mother House. The children of Calcutta had great needs. At Shishu Bhavan, Mother Teresa provided comfort to unlimited number of unwanted children, to orphans, sick, crippled or mentally handicapped, to those whose parents were unable to support them, to children whose mothers had died in Nirmal Hriday and to babies born to unmarried mothers, who would never be accepted back into their families. Children were cared for, fed, housed, clothed, taught and placed for adoption. Older children were sent to regular schools or taught a trade. Some were even married - married from the family of Mother Teresa and the sisters in the traditional custom of matchmaking. Within a decade, the Shishu Bhavans were established all over India and became the symbol of Mother Teresa's work. Although adoption remained an important part of the activities of these centres, many of them provided continuous care and a permanent home for hundreds of mentally retarded and severely handicapped children.

More than an orphanage, Shishu Bhavan is also an adoption center where abandoned children and infants find homes. Some of the hard-to-place children-the crippled, blind and retarded-may live their lives among the Missionaries of Charity.

Mary Ellen Mark, a New York-based writer and photographer visited Calcutta in 1980. While she was in Calcutta, Mark watched the nuns prepare a double wedding for two girls from the home. "The sisters dress the girls: polish is put on fingernails, powder and Indian makeup on their faces, henna on their feet. They wear red and white wedding saris and gold Jewelry-the nuns spent 5,000 rupees on each girl. The ceremony is a blend of Bengali and Catholic. Afterward Mother Teresa blesses them. People bring many gifts."

Giving in the most selfless way is the thing Mother Teresa knows most about. When asked about her life, she points to her work.

Though in the early days of the Missionaries of Charity the sisters begged-as much a symbol of humility and alliance with the poor as a mode of getting aid-Mother Teresa no longer solicits funds. "Money is no problem," she insists. "The Lord sends it. We do His work; He provides the means." And donations, from buildings to blankets to helping hands, always appear-though a bit of holy finagling helps.

Mark concluded, "Mother Teresa today is, as ever, dynamic, full of humor and utterly dedicated to helping the poor. Although she believes in praying, she says that prayer without action is no prayer at all. "You have to do your work as if everything depends on you." she says. "then leave the rest to God."

GANDHIJI PREM NIVAS

Mother Teresa was always concerned about the condition of leprosy patients. It was a widespread disease in the slums of Kolkata due to the unhygienic and the poor condition. In September, 1957 Mother Teresa laid the foundation for the first mobile leprosy clinic for the treatment of lepers, which was opened by Archbishop Perier at Shishu Bhavan on Lower Circular Road. Pope Paul VI donated an ambulance for carrying out the distribution of ration and free treatment to thousands of leprosy victims. An ambulance was also donated to her by Dr. Sen, an eminent specialist in leprosy treatment in Carmichael Hospital for Tropical Disease. The Sisters attended to patients distributing medicines and vitamins free of charge. Along the railway tracks of Titagarh, a suburb of Calcutta, there were ostracized, crime-ridden community of the leprosy afflicted. When they heard about Mother Teresa's mobile clinic, several leprosy families made weekly visits to the mobile dispensaries to get medicines. As the families found it difficult to commute, they begged Mother Teresa to open a clinic in Titagarh. Within a few months, she started with a mobile clinic under a tree near the Titagarh Municipal Sewage pumping station for treating a large group of leprosy patients. All kinds of medicines were provided, alongwith free distribution of milk and rice. But the clinic served only as pickle to feed an elephant. Considering the arduous task, Mother Teresa handed over the work to the Missionaries of Charity Brothers. The Brothers faced a lot of hardships. Some of the leper community, who did not like the changes, threw stones on the Brothers working along with them. However, the Brothers, along with pro-changers, built long and narrow barrack-like buildings. It consisted of a hospital, a cafeteria and small structures.

In 1958, she named the Titagarh Leprosy center as 'Gandhiji Prem Nivas', the 'Gandhi center for Love'. She had great respect for Gandhiji whom she called 'India's greatest soul'. The Gandhiji Prem Nivas Leprosy Centre, which stretches across a narrow 10-km strip along the Titagarh-Khardah railway line, providing free medical treatment for the patients and also taught them useful trades, such as carpentry, shoe-making and cloth weaving etc. These skills helped the lepers make a useful living and restored their human dignity.

Mother Teresa and her Sisters loved the lepers, touched them, treated them and provided them a dignified life. Mother Teresa created Shantinagar (Place for peace) for hundreds of leper families.

Seeing the dedication of Missionaries of Charity, numerous doctors and nurses gave free service and medical care in the leper-clinics. The Sisters at Missionaries of Charity never wore gloves to touch the maggot-ridden bodies of the dying because they felt that they were tending the body of Christ.

A society called 'Mariam Society' was then developed that included Indians, Anglo-Indians, Americans and other nationalists. They all helped Mother by forming working parties to make bandages and paper bags, in which the leper-pills could be distributed easily.

By the year 1984, four million leprosy patients were treated throughout mobile leprosy clinics, 1,06,271 people received weekly rations and 51,580 people got cooked food through the relief centers; 13,246 people were admitted to homes for dying destitute and 8,627 people were successfully discharged; otherwise, they might have died on the streets unwanted and uncared-for.

* * * * *

In 1960, after ten years in Calcutta, Mother Teresa was allowed to expand her work for the poor and needy beyond the Diocese of Calcutta. Any congregation less than ten years old was allowed to open a home outside the diocese. She went to the larger cities of India and opened charitable houses. Mother opened a home in Ranchi; within the next year opened three more homes in Delhi, Jhansi, and Agra. When Jawaharlal Nehru, the then Prime Minister of India, attended a ceremony dedicating a home for the needy children in Delhi, Mother Teresa asked him "Sir, shall I tell you about our work?", to which the Prime Minister replied very simply, "No, Mother, you need not tell me about your work. I know about it. That is why I have come".

By 1962, there were 52 relief centers and 6 dispensaries operated with the assistance of volunteer doctors and at 52 relief centers, food, milk and clothing collected by the Sisters are given to the needy. In the poorest districts of the city, the Sisters conduct regular day schools, under trees or a matting roof, teaching children to read and write in Hindi and do simple sums. This work was repeated in Delhi and six other cities. The Sisters also maintained a home in Delhi for orphans and retarded children.

In 1962, Mother Teresa's congregation numbered 169. Most of them were Indians, excepting few from Pakistan, Nepal, Malta, Albania, Yugoslavia, Germany, England and the United States. They lived as austerely as their slum neighbors. The Missionaries of Charity depended upon donations. Since 1956, the day of 29th January was set aside as Flag Day in the city of Calcutta, and men and women of many nationalities and creeds are seen in the streets, in offices, eating houses and at schools selling flags to help support the work of the Missionaries of Charity among the lepers. The symbol on the flag is a hand holding a clapper, recalling medieval times when lepers were outcasts in Europe, not allowed to live among their fellowmen, obliged to wear long white robes and masks over their faces, and to ring bells to warn of their approach, calling out "unclean, unclean." Over this symbol is written, "Touch the leper with your compassion." While the Sisters rendered selfless services to the poor, they made no attempts at conversion. They treated alike men of all castes, creeds and colors, concerned solely with injecting dignity into the lives of the unfortunate.

MISSIONARY BROTHERS OF CHARITY

During 1961, Sishu Bhavan had grown up boys. Mother Teresa realised that it would be difficulty for the Sisters to look after them. She thought that men could better handle heavier work and decided to start a congregation of Brothers. On March 25, 1963, the congregation of Missionary Brothers of Charity was founded under the inspired leadership of an Australian Jesuit, Father Ian Travers-Ball who with the approval of the order, left the Jesuits. Later he took up the name Brother Andrew. The religious habits of Brothers were white shirts and trousers. They do the same work and follow the same rigorous schedule as the women of the Missionaries of Charity. They stayed at Shishu Bhavan and got training from the Sisters. They also learnt carpentry. At first, the Brothers began to assist the Sisters in Titagarh. Later, when the Missionary Brothers of Charity got permission to function autonomously, they started their first work near Howarh Railway station. They helped the orphans and those suffering from infections and disease. However, the Brothers continued their involvement in leprosy work in Titagarh as well.

In the subsequent years, Brother Andrew spread the congregation of Brothers to many countries where they ran shelter for homeless, alcholic men and drug addicts. Some people from that place assisted the brothers in their work while some people came and saw if they could do the work. Brother Andrew coined an interesting phase for these people: "Come-and-Sees". Mother Teresa also adopted this name for the young women who wanted to see if they could do the work. The brothers had fourteen houses in 1975 with a staff of one hundred-fifty volunteers.

SHANTI NAGAR

Mother Teresa's had a dream to build a self-sufficient and treatment center for lepers. In the year 1961, the West Bengal government gave thirty-four acres of uncultivated land on lease to Mother Teresa. But, she had no funds to build the centers. In 1964, Pope Paul VI visited Bombay to participate in the International Eucharistic Congress. He used a custom-built Lincoln Continental limousine, which was specially flown in for his ride. He visited Mother Teresa's Home for the Dying in Bombay. He was so moved by the work rendered by the Missionaries of Charity. He gifted his ceremonial limousine to Mother Teresa before leaving India. Mother Teresa immediately raffled it and used the money to build a hospital. Subsequently, additional funds flowed in and soon her leper colony called Shanti Nagar (Town of Peace) was established. Many trees of bananas and palms were grown and few houses for leper families were built.

Within the next two years, essential buildings came up and Shanti Nagar, located near Asansol, 150 miles away from Calcutta, became an oasis for the lepers and their families. The leprosarium provided free medical treatment for the patients and also taught them useful trades, such as carpentry, shoe-making and cloth weaving etc. These skills helped the lepers make a useful living and restored their human dignity. A Shishu Bhavan was also built to take care of the children of the leprosy afflicted.

PREM DAN

It was started in 1973 in a godown donated by ICI and run by Sisters and novices. The inmates at Prem Dan were people who were suffering from malnutrition, tuberculosis, various kinds of physical handicaps, mental problems and cancer. Like all Mother Teresa's centres, Prem Dan is clean, and enveloped with an air of calm.

LINK FOR SICK AND SUFFERING CO-WORKERS

This society came into existence when Jacqueline de Decker, a Belgian woman met with Mother Teresa in December 1948. Jacqueline belonged to a wealthy business family in Antwerp. She was a trained nurse and had rendered invaluable medical service to the prisoners of war. Like Mother Teresa, Jacqueline had also felt a 'Call of inner self' at the age of 17 that she wanted to serve India's poor. When she heard about Mother Teresa's work, she wanted to join her. She first met Mother Teresa at Patna and came to know one another well. Mother Teresa invited her to join her in the work that she proposed to begin in Calcutta. Jacqueline readily expressed her willingness. As she was suffering with a severe disease of the spine, she had to return to Antwerp for treatment. She underwent a series of surgeries, which prevented her travel back to India to join Mother Teresa in her work. But Mother Teresa's inspiring and beautiful letters made Jacqueline spiritually attached to Mother Teresa's new Congregation, the Missionaries of Charity. Mother wanted the paralyzed, the crippled or aged to join the Missionary of Charity by totally surrendering to

God. She thought and offered a two-way solution. The sick and suffering co-workers were each linked with a particular Missionary of Charity Sister or Brother. They offered only their pain and agony and prayed for the work. In turn, the active Brother or Sister worked with renewed energy and prayed for them. They called each other their 'second self'. Mother Teresa was linked to Jacqueline as her 'second self'. And thus, in January 1953, she formed the 'Sick and Suffering Co-Workers'.

In this manner, through the Link for Sick and Suffering Co-Workers, Mother with efficiency and perfection, achieved two goals:- one was the need for a kind of power house of prayer on the part of her Missionaries of Charity and the other was the need of the sick and suffering to find a meaning to their existence. Mother Teresa later explained to one of her biographers, Navin Chawla, "the Suffering Co-Workers are sick persons who adopt one of our Sisters. If you are sick, and you have got me and you offer all your pain and all your suffering for me, you offer that to God for me, for the work I do. And I offer the work, and my love of God for you. I help you and you help me. And we other become selves to each other. It is a tremendous gift. You cannot go out to work, so I do the working and you do the suffering. I have a person who does that for me, she (Jacqueline) has had so many operations already. She offers every operation for me, while I go running about the place for her. She is in terrible pain but she offers everything for me. We have an understanding that we share everything together. That is the bond. She, with suffering, I with work and prayers. Beautiful. Every Sister has a sick person praying for her."

On 26 March 1969, the International Association of Co-workers of Mother Teresa was recognized by the Vatican. According to its constitution, 'co-workers are men, women, young people and children of all religion and denominations throughout the world who seek to love God in their fellowmen through whole–hearted service to the poorest of the poor of all castes and creeds. They wish to unite themselves in a spirit of prayer and sacrifice with the work of Mother Teresa and Missionaries of Charity.' Jacqueline was named the International Link for the Sick and Suffering. She performed her task for nearly three decades. According to Navin Chawla's book, Jacqueline de Decker stepped down from the organization in the year 1995, as she was no longer able to continue the work. Sister Anand, a German nun of the Missionaries of Charity took over the work.

Mother Teresa shared her spirit of prayer, simplicity, sacrifice and her apostolate of humble works of love with the Co-workers and Sick and Suffering Co-workers of many faiths and nationalities.

During the month of April 1965, Mother Theresa was in Rome anxious to promote the status of the Missionaries of Charity from being a diocesan congregation to being a congregation with formal papal approval, a congregation of pontifical status. At an audience with Pope John XXIII she wanted to ask this favour of him when surprisingly she lost her nerve. However, on 2 May 1965 she duly received the recognition she had desired through the Cardinal in charge of missionary work.

When Mother Teresa was granted permission to open missions outside India, she was invited by the Bishop of Venezuela to come and see the plight of landless community. She decided to open her first mission in Cocorote, Venezuela in South America. Her Sisters in Calcutta opened an atlas to locate the place. Mother Teresa, observing them with amusement, said, "If there are poor people on the moon, we will go there'.

On 26 July 1965 Mother Teresa established her first mission in Venezuela and the Missionaries of Charity became a world congregation. Sister Nirmala, the present Superior General of Missionaries of Charity was a pioneer of the first foundation outside India in Venezuela.

CONTEMPLATIVE SISTERS

In June 25, 1976, Mother Teresa began a Contemplative branch of the Missionaries of Charity Sisters under the direction of Sister Nirmala. The mission of the Contemplative Sisters is to go in search of the souls of the poorest of the poor through the apostolate of prayer, in particular Eucharistic adoration, and the spiritual works of mercy.

CONTEMPLATIVE BROTHERS

In March 19, 1979, the Contemplative Brothers, a branch of Missionaries of Charity was formed by Mother

Teresa alongwith Fr. Sebastian Vazhakala, in answer to a similar desire of men for a more contemplative life in the service of the poor. It was formally established as a Diocesan Congregation in Rome on 8 December, 1993.

CORPUS CHRISTI MOVEMENT

Mother Teresa had a great love and reverence for the priesthood. In answer to the requests of many priests, in June 26, 1981 Mother Teresa, with the help of Fr. Joseph Langford, formed the Corpus Christi Movement for Priests as a "little way of holiness" for those who desire to share in her charisma and spirit.

MISSIONARIES OF CHARITY FATHERS

Mother Teresa along with Fr. Joseph Langford, formed the Missionaries of Charity Fathers on 31 October 1984. Their purpose is to give priestly service to the poorest of the poor, spiritual assistance to the Missionaries of Charity Family, and to spread Mother Teresa's spirituality and mission. The Fathers became a congregation of diocesan right in Tijuana, Mexico in 1992.

The Missionaries of Charity Brothers and Fathers are separate congregations from the sisters but share the same spirit and vow of wholehearted free service to the poorest of the poor. The Brothers report to the General Servant (the head of their order), or to their regional superiors. The Fathers report to their Superior General.

The Missionaries of Charity Brothers have a two-year novitiate after an initial trial period lasting from three to six months. There is no obligatory postulant period for the brothers. The brothers are more active, doing similar work to that of the sisters.

The Fathers are more contemplative, praying and saying Mass. They are either already ordained priests or those training to be priests with the Missionaries of Charity.

LAY MISSIONARIES OF CHARITY

In April 21, 1987, Mother Teresa formed the Lay Missionaries of Charity with the help of Father Sebastian Vazhakala. Its purpose is 'to sanctify themselves and their own families by consecrating themselves, their families and the whole world entirely to God after the example of Jesus, Mary and Joseph and practice the same virtues they practised'. The Lay Missionaries of Charity is now an International Association of Lay people: married and single who adhering to the Spirit and Charism of the Missionaries of Charity Family make private (juridically) vows of Chastity (conjugal), Poverty, Obedience and the fourth vow of Whole-Hearted Free Service to the poorest of the poor beginning with the members of one's own family. Remaining in the heart of the world, the LMCs consecrate the world itself to God everywhere offering worship by the holiness of their lives expressed through prayer, penance and works of mercy, after the example of the Holy Family of Nazareth.

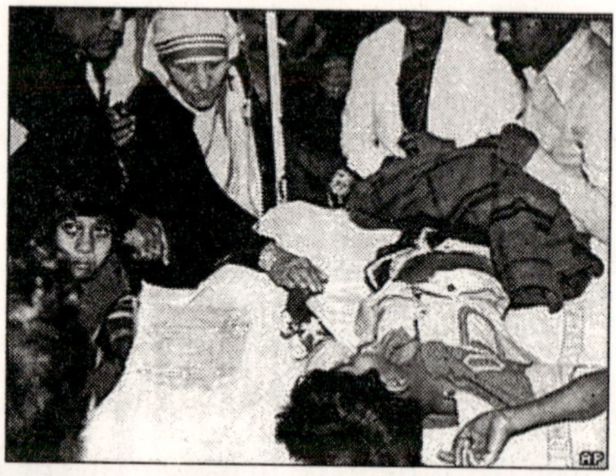

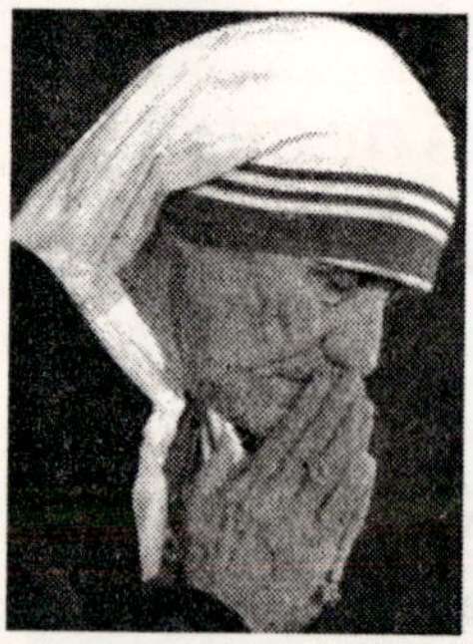

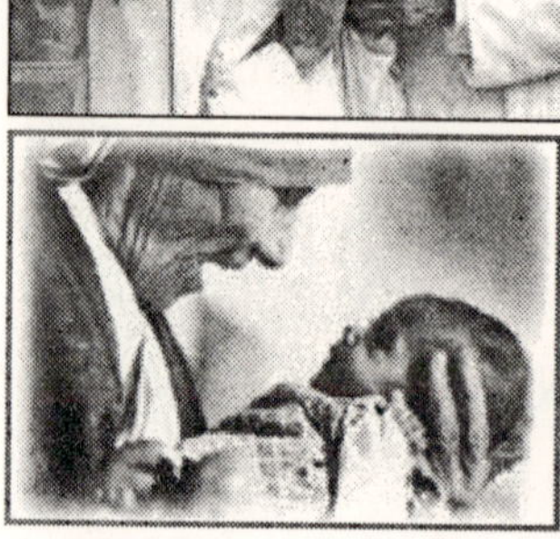

5

INTERNATIONAL CONTRIBUTION

Mother Teresa's first home outside India was opened on 26 July 1965 in Venezuela. Mother Teresa left for Venezuela with five Sisters to work within South American culture, training and teaching especially the woman about their own dignity and practical skills. They opened a house there for giving free services to the poor, sick, conducted funeral services, washed and cleaned the old and fed the hungry.

In 1968 she was summoned to Rome to set up a home there, staffed primarily with Indian nuns. The Sisters settled in a very small house amongst city's poor worked in the slum areas. They helped the refugees from Sicily and Sardinia teaching them skilled work.

The same year, Mother Teresa was in Tanzania, the land of her dreams of childhood. Subsequently, she was invited to visit Australia and help the drug-addicts, alcoholics, prisoners who were in need of rehabilitation and young teenagers crying for love and affection.

In July, 1970, Mother Teresa and her five Sisters helped a large number of refuges living in pathetic conditions in camps in Jordon. The same year she visited London and shocked to see people sleeping under the tarpaulins and many people were staying under the railway arches. She started a house in London for these homeless people. The Missionaries of Charity also opened Homes of Compassion for deserted men and women, knocked on the doors of the isolated and old people and touched areas of human suffering, which others neglected.

On January 4, 1970, Mother Teresa received a sad letter from her sister, Age, telling her mother's health was deteriorating and wished to meet Mother Teresa again before her death. She visited Belgrade on the invitation of Yugoslavian Red Cross and was very close to her home. But due to political reasons, she could not enter Albania to meet her mother and sister. Later on July 12, 1972, Drana Bojaxhiu died in Arans, Albania. Her sister, Age also died on August 25, 1973 in Tirana.

In the month of October in the same year, Bangladesh was hit by one of the worst and disastrous cyclones, leaving more than 300,000 people dead. Mother Teresa and her sisters rushed to help the people.

During the Bangladesh Liberation War in 1971, 300,000 lives were lost in the war. More than 200,000 women were raped and millions of people were homeless. Their lives were in terrible conditions. The Bangladesh government requested Mother Teresa to help the victims of war. She rushed with two teams of Missionaries of Charity and set up one house in Dhaka and many more in Bangladesh. She also opened many dispensaries and provided medical care to pregnant women. She gave hope to the helpless. She taught the women to make puffed rice, which they could sell in the market to feed their children.

The Missionaries of Charity also set up their simple Convent in the centre of South Bronx area of New York in 1971. The Sisters helped the children, visited the lonely, sick and the unwanted. The same year, Mother and her four Sisters visited Belfast, a place full of hatred and unlawful acts. They worked there in association with a small group of Anglican nuns. They quietly helped the local people and their children.

In 1972, the costal areas Venezuela was hit by cyclone and a large number of people became homeless. The Sisters helped the people in repairing their homes.

The Indian Government made her travelling and movement very easy and granted Mother Teresa all kinds of visa facilities and free from custom duties. She was given innumerable concessions like free travel on Indian Railways etc. In 1973, Indira Gandhi gave her a free pass on Indian Airlines so that she could keep in touch with her various Missionary of Charity homes throughout the world.

Mother with her Sisters, in 1973, went to Ethiopia to reach out to the victims of a dreadful drought in Northern Ethiopia.

When Mother Teresa wanted to set up a house in Ethiopia, she was warned that it would not be easy. But, Mother Teresa had abundant faith that God would guide her in her mission. She sought an audience with the Emperor Haile Selassie, but the Minister of the Imperial Court intercepted her. He asked what they were going to do, as a great famine had hit the country and men, women and children were dying of malnutrition. Mother Teresa replied, "We give wholehearted free service to the poorest of the poor' But, the Minister demanded, "What qualifications do you have?", Without a moment of hesitation, Mother replied, "We bring love and compassion to the people'. The Minister was convinced by her replies and granted an audience with Emperor Selassie, who was moved by Mother Teresa's work allowed her Sisters to come to Ethiopia.

Mother Teresa set up a home for unwanted children, paralyzed young adults and old men and women in Peru. The Missionaries of Charity Brothers took care of hundreds of unsheltered people, crippled, disabled and retarded. The same year, Mother Teresa went to Gaza to help the people living in Israeli occupied territory. They struggled to remove the fear and sorrow of people who had lost hope.

By 1973, Mother had established the Sisters foundations in Jordan, England, the United States,

Bangladesh, Mauritius, Israel, the Yemen, Peru, and various other places.

In June, 1976, in New York, Cardinal Cooke, in Mother's presence, blessed the new branch of Missionaries of Charity. Sister Nirmala was made the leader of this new branch. At first, the branch, was known as 'Sisters of the Word' but later in 1977, it was renamed 'Missionaries of Charity, Contemplative.' In 1977, Mother Teresa and her Sisters helped two million people who were left homeless due to a devastating cyclone. Several thousands people died. In 1978, Mother Teresa established a branch for men in a slum area of Rome. The branch was also called 'Brothers of the Word' under the Roman prelate.

By 1978, Mother's work was internationally recognized and her message of love spread widely. She was invited by the Catholic bishops to visit Yugoslavia. On March 28, 1978, Mother visited Yugoslavia. Skopje, her hometown welcomed her royally and joyfully. She opened a house in Skopje as well as in Zagreb.

In the late 1970s the Missionaries of Charity numbered more than 1,000 nuns who operated 60 centres in Calcutta and more than 200 worldwide centres, including foundations in Sri Lanka, Tanzania, Jordan, Venezuela, Great Britain, and Australia. Though Mother Teresa then traveled frequently outside India, her soul was with each of the Sisters at Calcutta.

In April, 1981, Mother visited Japan at the invitation of the "Japan Family Life Association". On May 24, the same year, she opened a house of the Missionaries of Charity, in Sanya district of Tokyo, that was famous for the number of alcoholics who met there. The Missionaries of Charity opened eight more foundations in India and another seventeen in America, Europe, Africa, Australia, and Asia including a house in Tokyo and one more house in the Iron country, Germany's the then East Berlin. By the year, 1981, she had opened twenty-six houses, eighteen of them outside India.

Mother Teresa visited Cincinnati on June 7, 1981, to help the Franciscan community there to launch a year-long celebration of the 800th anniversary of the birth of St. Francis of Assisi. Although there was no direct connection between Mother Teresa's order and the Franciscan orders, she was known as a great admirer of St. Francis of Assisi. Accordingly, her influence and life show influences of Franciscan spirituality. Her sisters say the peace prayer of St. Francis every morning before breakfast and many of the vows and emphasis of her ministry are similar. St. Francis emphasized poverty, chastity, obedience and submission to Christ. He also devoted much of his own life to service of the poor, especially lepers in the area where he lived.

While talking with a small group of Franciscans, Pentecost, Mother Teresa said why she admires St. Francis and the impact on her life. "I suppose it's because St. Francis of Assisi tried to imitate the poverty of Christ so closely", she said. The incident in the life of St. Francis that most appealed to her was his kissing of the leper. One day St. Francis had passed a leper on the road—too repulsed at first even to greet the man. "But then he came back and embraced him," Mother

Teresa relates. "That was the beginning of St. Francis. That act of surrender made St. Francis.... After that he was ready to give anything!"

Some of Mother Teresa's fascination with St. Francis was more lighthearted: "I love St. Francis of Assisi," she said, breaking into her famous smile, "because he had a great love for animals. He used to talk with them and play with them—and scold them if they did harm to anybody. I love animals, too. Animals are such simple creations of God's beauty."

Mother Teresa also recalled with some delight how St. Clare of Assisi was inducted into the Franciscan family. Clare had stolen away from her wealthy family one night and came to Francis and the friars to have her beautiful golden hair cut off as a sign of her new commitment. "They cut her hair quickly, quickly," Mother Teresa said with mischievous enjoyment—snipping her fingers in the air, "so nobody would want to take her back home!"

Meanwhile, on July 3, 1981, Lazar Bojaxhiu, Mother Teresa's brother, died of cancer of the lungs in Palermo, Italy. Mother could never meet her family members and that regret always remained with her. But she vowed to herself that she would do something for her birthplace, to bring peace and love among the people of Albania.

Mother Teresa's love for poor made her known throughout the world. Her work made a strong impact on people all around the world. In her respect, over a hundred thousand school children in Denmark go without a glass of milk everyday, so that others might eat. Eight hundred thousand capsules of Lampren were sent annually from Switzerland to the lepers in West Bengal. At Mother Teresa's request, five thousand tonnes of high-quality processed food was dispatched at a week's notice for the famine-hit people of Ethiopia and Tanzania.

In 1982, Mother Teresa persuaded Israelis and Palestinians, who were in the midst of a skirmish, to cease fire long enough to rescue 37 mentally handicapped patients from a besieged hospital in Beirut.

In December, 1983, another house was opened in East Germany, in Karl Marx. Mother believed that poverty of the people in communist countries was worse than any other country. The people were devoid of the knowledge of the love of God for all men. Despite her weak body, she wanted to remove this poverty by knowledge and love.

Mother had a dream of visiting China in 1984. The Chinese government being communist discouraged her in the beginning but at her repeated request to bring a little hope and encouragement in the heart of depressed people, the government allowed her to visit China. In 1984, she visited Poland instead of China. At the end of 1984, Africa was hit by famine. She left for Ethiopia despite her poor health condition. She organized wide spread famine relief centers.

Mother considered AIDS as another form of poverty and the victims of AIDS as the 'lepers of the West'. In 1985, she set out to open a hospital in the Greenwich village at the East side of Manhattan for people who were victims of AIDS and whose family and friends had thrown them, leaving them to fend for themselves and to face a terrible and painful death.

The new hospital she established in New York was called 'Gift of Love'. It was very much the same like Nirmal Hriday of Calcutta. Here the people can die in peace and felt that they are being loved.

But Mother and her Sisters faced with a common problem while working with dying AIDS patients similar to that of Nirmal Hriday of Calcutta. People who lived in the neighborhood of the AIDS hospital vehemently opposed. Despite the opposition, she went on to open her second home for the victims of AIDS and other terminal diseases. On June 13, 1986, she met the United States President, Ronald Reagan at the White House and got approval to open her second home for AIDS victims.

Archbishop of Washington invited Mother Teresa to open a new home. Upon accepting his invitation, she established the 'Gift of Peace' home. It was not as much a hospital but a 'loving home where person with AIDS and other terminal diseases could come and find the care, compassion and peace they deserved as children of God.'

Later on, Georgetown University Medical College joined the homes and provided all types of medical help to the patients. Finally on November 8, 1986, the 'Gift of Peace' was opened amidst opposition and angry demonstrations by the neighbors and other people.

Despite many awareness campaign and literature on AIDS, people were not convinced and the Missionaries of Charity Sisters faced obstacles in their work of trying to bring love and care to the suffering people. Mother was determined and continued to spread her message that AIDS should be seen as 'a sign that God wants us to open our hearts and love for one another'.

The work with AIDS patients grew at a faster pace. In June, 1988, another Gift of Love was opened in San Francisco, and in March, 1989 a similar Gift of Love was opened in Addis Ababa, Ethiopia. In December, 1989, an AIDS home was started by the Sisters in Denver, Colorado.

AIDS crisis busted in Los Angeles and Brothers were particularly doing a great work there. One of the Brothers, started a day care facility in Oakland, the first of its kind in the country where the AIDS victims were welcomed with their families and people who tried to care for the victims. The medical Co-Workers and Missionaries of Charity provided every possible help to the Brothers so that the suffering of the 'Leprosy of the West' (AIDS) could be lessened.

In October 1986, after the opening of 'Gift of Peace' home in Washington, Mother reached the famine-affected people of Sudan and planned to open up a centre in the south to care for some of the victims. In Khartoum, she prayed for the victims of the three-year-old civil war in Southern Sudan.

In November, 1988, Mother finally visited South Africa. Even though political tension was prevailing at that time, she was given an ecstatic welcome. With an extraordinary pace, Mother achieved whatever she wanted in that racial town and left it giving obvious joy to people living at the edge of gang-wars and political fighting. She tried to bring some smiles on these suffering people. On December 7, a killer earthquake in Armenia caused the death of about fifty-five thousand people. More than ten thousand people were treated in hospitals and many more were left homeless. Following the catastrophic earthquake, a special Prime Minister's Armenia Earthquake Relief Fund was constituted in India, which donated US$ 2.2 million and US$ 1.1 million relief supplies. An Indian medical team visited Armenia for relief work. Mother immediately left for Armenia. She visited the children's hospital where they were taken care of. She set up a still functioning orphanage in the earthquake-hit city of Spitak. She spent time with each child praying for them and giving them miraculous medals. Her presence brought a renewed hope in the hearts of people who had lost their loved ones. On December 15, the same year, Mother Teresa was invited by the Soviet Peace Committee in Moscow to come to the then USSR to open a house in Moscow.

Gradually, Mother was taking over all the communist countries under her grace and love. Her achievements were unending, especially opening foundations and home in politically disturbed countries, and was seen as a milestone in the history of charity work. She was invited by Czechoslovakia in 1988. She received a warm welcome in the township of Nita, in central Czechoslovakia. She opened two houses there, which attracted people in large numbers to welcome the arrival of the Sisters in their white saris.

She had another dream of setting up a Missionary of Charity foundation in Albania, which was the poorest European country. It was under the communist regime, who were 'Legally atheist' and had banned religious practices. Since 1967, over two thousand places of worship were closed down. Most of them were mosques and former catholic churches were used as sports stadium and for other official purposes.

The catholic churches were the primary targets for closing down as they put resistance to communism. Building a church was impossible in Albania. Parents as well as children were banished from praying or keeping Bibles in their homes and school. As in Romania, forty years of communism removed basic moral and spiritual values and in this way, God was effectively thrown out of Albania.

Mother Teresa who had been battling quietly against communism for a long time wanted to bring her Jesus back into her homeland, Albania. And finally in May 1990, Albania's communist regime lifted the twenty-three-years old ban and people were allowed to follow religious work.

Mother Teresa approached the President of Albania, Mr. Ramiz Alia, to bring Sisters to Albania who would bring tender love and care for the Albanians. By February 1992, she was given permission to bring her Sisters to Albania. Mother and her Sisters were given warm welcome. Everyday, large crowds gathered at the new house opened by the Sisters. Being physically weak and old, she greeted them and gave her blessings. She told them, "We have come to give tender love and care, as we do throughout the world. We will begin slowly and see what is the greatest need." She brought some more Sisters from Rome to Albania and opened three more houses: two for Tirana and one for Shkoder. The Tirana houses were home for the destitute, sick people and Shkoder was home for abandoned, crippled and mentally retarded children. Mother also opened the Tirana's Cathedral Church of the Sacred Heart. Thousands of people took part in the first Mass, which was celebrated after a long ban on religion. She was requested by the President to open six churches, which she did happily. She also reopened a mosque for the Muslims too. The Muslims saw the Sisters and Mother sweeping and cleaning the floors of the mosque, which resulted into better Muslim-Christian relations in the new democratic Albania.

Mother's Albania visit helped to reinstate the status of religion in the country. Earlier attempts made by Pope Johan Paul II to resolve the broken relationship with Albania were failed in May 1945. Mother Teresa renewed the relation through her Missionaries of Charity in September 1991.

After her long and tiring but happy journey to Albania, she went back to Rome on April 20, 1991 suffering from severe cough. But she was determined to go to Romania leaving her bad health aside. She wanted to see as to how the Sisters of those three new houses for handicapped and retarded children were growing. All the children were developing fast under the care and love of the sisters. Mother's appearances on Romania's television showing how she and her sisters were working, gave a spectacular rise in the number of girls joining the Missionaries of Charity. Meanwhile, she opened houses in Cambodia and in Vietnam.

Before the Gulf War, she had written a letter to both President George Bush and Saddam Hussein appealing to them to choose the way of peace. She begged on behalf of the innocent ones, the poor of the world and of those who would become poor after the War. In 1992, she got the message that she would be welcomed by Iraq to bring hope to many sufferers. Mother could not say 'no' to the cries of many hopeless and homeless people. During the 'Operation Desertstorm', thousands of people were killed, many more left homeless, wounded or hungry. When all Brothers and Sisters were busy in America for getting ready for parades and festivities, Mother and Sisters were heading towards Baghdad. On June 11, Mother and her two Sisters arrived at Baghdad from Switzerland. Though the welcome was a very warm one but the scenes that waited for them were horrible. Mother was deeply affected by the horror of War. She asked everybody, "the fruit of War is so terrible, one cannot understand how any human being can do that to another – and for what?" After a meeting with the Health Minister, she got clear information about the medical and humanitarian needs of Iraq and arranged to rebuild the homes destroyed in war.

In 2001, some 4,000 Sisters of the Missionaries of Charity, clad in white saris with blue borders, were pursuing her rigorous path, along with 450 Brothers in a separate men's order. Mother Teresa had created a network of 569 missions spread across 120 nations that operated workshops for the unemployed, food centers, orphanages, leprosariums, and refuges for the insane, retarded and aged.

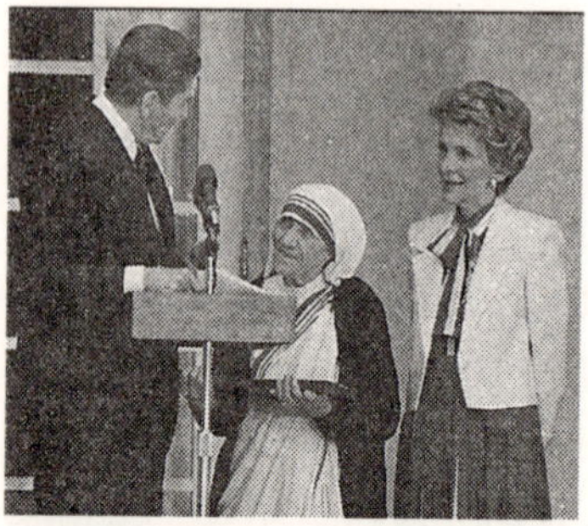

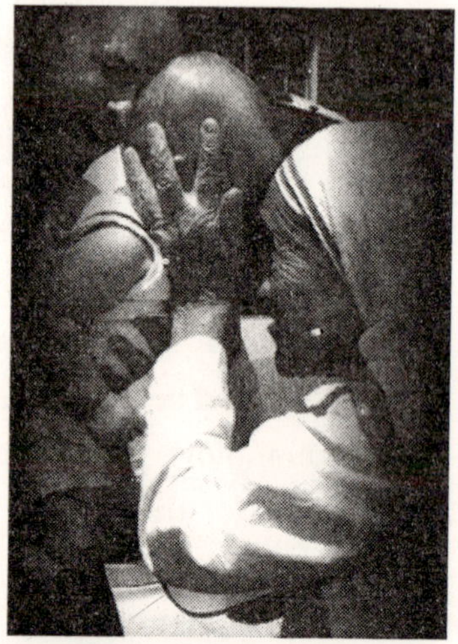

1894 - 1995

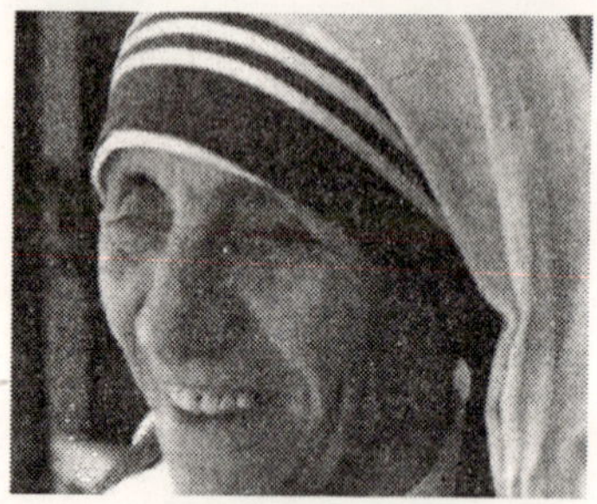

6

Awards and Recognition

Mother Teresa was recognized all over the world and she received many awards. It was in 1962, after fourteen years Mother Teresa began her work in the slums, she was recognized for the first time. The Indian government honoured her with India's second highest award, the 'Padma Shri'. She received the award from the then President of India, Dr. Rajendra Prasad. When congratulated her response bespoke the firm faith, which was her guide: "But what have I done? It is His work and I simply follow."

In the same year in August, Mother Teresa received the Ramon Magsaysay Award for International Understanding in recognition of her merciful cognizance of the abject poor in India, in whose service she had led a new congregation. While receiving the award on 31 August 1962 in Manila, Philippines, Mother Teresa said:

"I am very happy to be here today, to join with you in thanking God to have given to the world, torn with suffering, a man like Ramon Magsaysay, who loved and served his people so well. This award which is given to me and through me to the young Congregation, to the countless benefactors and to our poor in India, will be a new source of encouragement for us to love and serve the poor as Ramon Magsaysay did with our whole heart and soul.

Our Congregation is totally dedicated to the Service of the Poor, to serve Christ in His distressing disguise. Therefore our home for the dying, the home for the crippled and unwanted children, our care of lepers, our slum schools, our clinics, all come from that Source and aim at the same idea, to give wholehearted free Service to the Poor for the Love of God." Along with the Ramon Magsaysay Award, she was given a cheque of Rs. 50,000. She utilized this award money to buy the Children's Home in Agra.

In January 1971, Mother Teresa won the Pope John XXIII Peace Prize in Rome and she was awarded with a cheque worth £10,000. She donated the prize money for construction of a leper colony in Madhya Pradesh. In the same year, she was also honoured with the Joseph Kennedy Junior Foundation Award followed by Good Samaritan Prize, Boston. In November 1972, the Indian government gave her the 'Nehru Award for International Understanding' for inspiring a large number of devoted people all over the world to work with her in the service of the destitute, the uncared and helpless people of the society. In the same year, she also received the 'Koruna Dut Award' (Angel of Charity) from the President of India, who said," "Mother Teresa is one of those liberated souls who have transcended all barriers presented by race, religion, and nationality. In our present-day troubled world, incessantly plagued by conflict and hatred, the life that is lived and the work that is carried out by people like Mother Teresa bring new hope for the future of mankind"

In 1973, the first Templeton Prize was awarded to Mother Teresa. The Templeton Prize for Progress in Religion committee recognized her extraordinary efforts to help the homeless and neglected children of Calcutta; for her heroic work which not only affected real change among those she served, but inspired millions of others around the world. She was selected out of a total of two thousand nominations by a panel of judges representing the major religious traditions of the world.

In 1974, she received the Mater et Magistra Award. On October 23, 1975, she became one of the recipients of the first Albert Schweitzer International Prizes, awarded at the University of North Carolina, Washington.

In 1979, when Mother Teresa was told that she had been nominated for Nobel Prize for Peace, her reaction was, "I am unworthy'. The Norwegian Nobel Committee awarded the Nobel Peace Prize to Mother Teresa 'for work undertaken in the struggle to overcome poverty and distress, which also constitute a threat to peace.' On December 10, 1979, in the presence of King Olaf V, Crown Prince Harald, Crown Princess Sonja, and many other dignitaries, Mother accepted the Nobel Prize for Peace and the money, as she had accepted all other honors 'in the name of poor, the hungry, the sick and the lonely'. The Chairman of the Norwegian Nobel Committee, in his presentation speech said, 'The hallmark of her work has been respect for the individual and the individual's worth and dignity. The loneliest and the most wretched, the dying destitute, the abandoned lepers, have been received by her and her Sisters with warm compassion devoid of condescension, based on this reverence for Christ in Man...... She believes that the worst disease today is not leprosy or tuberculosis, but rather the feeling of being unwanted, uncared for and deserted by everybody.... Her intention was to ensure that they enjoyed the feeling of being received and recognised as people with their own human dignity and the right to respect.' He concluded, 'There would be no better way of describing the intentions that have motivated the decision of the Norwegian Nobel Committee than the comment of the President of the World Bank, Robert MacNamara, when he declared: "Mother Teresa deserves Nobel's Peace Prize because she promotes peace in the most fundamental manner, by her confirmation of the inviolability of human dignity'.

In her acceptance speech, Mother Teresa said: 'There is so much suffering, so much hatred, so much misery, and we with our prayer, with our sacrifice are beginning at home. Love begins at home, and it is not how much we do, but how much love we put in the action that we do.'

She refused the conventional ceremonial banquet given to laureates, and asked that the $7,000 funds be diverted to the poor in Calcutta, claiming the money would permit her to feed hundreds of needy for a year. When Mother Teresa received the prize, she was asked, "What can we do to promote world peace?" Her answer was simple: "Go home and love your family. In the same year she won Balzan Prize for promoting 'peace and brotherhood among nations'.

In 1980, the then President of India, Neelam Sanjiva Reddy, gave her India's highest civilian award, the 'Bharat Ratna'. On November 24, 1983, Mother was presented with the insignia of the Honorary Order of Merit, by Queen Elizabeth II at the Presidential Palace in Delhi.

On June 20, 1985, at the White House in Washington, the then U.S. President, Ronald Reagan presented her with the United States Presidential Medal of Freedom, calling her a 'heroine of our times'. In 1992, she was conferred with the title 'Bharat ki Suputri ('the great daughter of India'). In 1993, she was honoured with Rajiv Gandhi Sadbhavana Award. In 1994, the President of Albania, Mr. Ramiz Alia, awarded the citizenship of Albania to Mother Teresa, who had once been forced to take a sad decision of not visiting her dying mother in her homeland.

On May 16, 1997, she was awarded by the United States, a Congressional gold medal in recognition of her "outstanding and enduring contributions to humanitarian and charitable activities".

Mother Teresa received many awards and honours that one could find it difficult to compile a complete list. Navin Chawla, in his book, wrote, 'For a woman who never went to university, Mother Teresa held a string of honorary doctorates conferred on her by some of the most prestigious universities.'

On March 3, 1976, the Vishwa Bharti University, West Bengal, conferred on Mother Teresa the University's highest honor, 'The Deshikottama' (Doctorate of Literature). Indira Gandhi, the then Prime Minister of India, commented on her, "She is tiny to look at, but there is nothing small about her." In June 1977, She was awarded an honorary Doctorate of Divinity by the University of Cambridge. In 1982, the Catholic University of Brussels awarded her an honorary doctorate. In 1988, she received an honorary degree of Humane Letters from the University of San Diego. Harvard University also awarded her their honorary doctorate amidst an unprecedented standing ovation. In 1984, she received an honorary doctorate of Law from the University of Madras. Innumerable magazine nominated her 'Woman of the Year' in their annual polls and was voted as the 'Most Admired Woman' in the world. She adorned postage stamps in Sweden and in India. Numerous awards were honoured on her from all over the world, but she remained unperturbed, her own true self. She walked with Kings, Presidents and Prime Ministers of many countries, but never lost the common touch that came naturally to her.

While she earned international respect for her work in the form of awards and honours, Mother Teresa also attracted criticisms. She was accused of exploiting her fame, accepting funding from questionable sources and refusing to give any account of the money she received in donations. She and her Sisters were accused of secretly converting the patients to Catholic faith who were brought to her homes. There were charges that her sisters not only give succor to the dying but also asked if they wanted 'tickets to heaven,' secretly baptizing lifelong Hindus and Muslims to Catholic faith. Once Mother was asked what her reaction was to this criticism. She replied, 'Yes, I do. I convert Hindus to be better Hindus and Muslims to be better Muslims'

Apart from this, Mother Teresa had a more controversial side: she was never afraid to speak and act with impunity on matters of the secular world. Mother Teresa's vehement opposition to abortion and contraception, stemming from the rigid Catholic 'pro-life' position, was one that troubled many people, including those who supported her activities the world over. She was always against abortion and sterilization. She did not accept the programme of sterilization in India under Indira Gandhi's rule. For her, even a leper has every right to give birth. While receiving an honorary Doctorate of Medicine from Rome's Catholic University in December 1981, she said, 'Abortion is nothing but the fear of the child—— fear to have to feed one more child, to have to educate one more child, to have to love one more child. Therefore, the child must die.' She repeatedly decried abortion wherever she had the opportunity. "If a mother can kill her own child, then what is left of the West to be destroyed?" she once said. According to her, abortion was 'the greatest evil'.

Mother Teresa's views on abortion and sterilization have had many detractors. Social scientists had often stridently pointed out to her that several countries where she worked had massive population problems, and these were unlikely to go away by her simply offering to take in all unwanted children. There are many who argued that Mother Teresa should have used her very considerable influence to propagate birth control. To this Mother Teresa firmly replied that she advocated 'natural family planning', involving abstention by couples, and called for the exercise of self-control. Mother Teresa believed that this method involved 'love and respect for one another', and that this had, over the years, successfully averted thousands of births. Natural family planning cannot, of course, be expected to apply to unwed mothers or girls forced into prostitution. Nor did Mother Teresa have a very convincing answer to the problems of the pressures on most Indian families, and indeed, in most conservative societies, when faced with the prospect of an unmarried mother in their midst. In such countries, a child born to an unmarried girl would not merely bring shame to the immediate family but disgrace to an entire village or community.

None of this deterred Mother Teresa. She had implicit faith in the Roman Catholic doctrine of birth control and abhorred the word 'abortion'. There were innumerable occasions, particularly on her visits to the United States and Europe, when she spoke up against it. In her Nobel Lecture itself, which she delivered in Oslo in 1979, she said that she believed that the greatest destroyer of peace was not war but abortion. Abortion was a 'direct war', murder committed by the mother herself.

During the fortieth anniversary celebrations of the United Nations, a film on Mother Teresa was screened. At the conclusion of the film, Mother Teresa, who was present, made a brief speech. She spoke about alove and sharing and the need to bring prayer back in our lives. 'We are frightened of nuclear war, we are frightened of this terrible new disease, AIDS, but we are not frightened to kill an innocent child. Today I feel that abortion has become the greatest destroyer of peace.' These views made many in the audience uncomfortable. Many felt that Mother Teresa should speak against abortion, as her organization worked mostly in over-populated countries.

Mother Teresa was, of course, perfectly aware that her views on abortion were not widely shared and that most governments, the press and the intelligentsia did not support them. She also knew that other religious denominations did not always take a rigid stand against abortion. She was certainly aware that many Catholic organizations failed to agree with her; time and time again, polls in America and Europe revealed that a majority of Catholics favoured contraception and abortion under exceptional circumstances. None of this caused her to amend her beliefs in the slightest.

In 1980, she unsuccessfully led a campaign in Ireland against a law, which would permit civil divorce and remarriage. A few months later, she gave an interview to the American magazine, Ladies Home Journal, which reached millions of housewives. During the interview, she was asked about her friendship with Princess Diana, a friendship, which has been evolving over the past several years, and also about Diana's then impending divorce. Of the divorce, Mother Teresa said that, 'It is a good thing that it is over. Nobody was happy anyhow'.

She was undeterred by criticism about her firm stand against abortion and divorce saying, "No matter who says what, you should accept it with a smile and do your own work."

In 1994 Britain's Channel 4 broadcasted a revisionist look at Mother Teresa that was harshly titled 'Hell's Angel'. Written by Pakistani-born leftist Tariq Ali and British columnist Christopher Hitchens, the program claimed that the Missionaries of Charity accepted donations from some disreputable figures like Jean-Claude Duvalier, the deposed Haitian dictator. Mother Teresa replied that she had no moral right to refuse donations given for the poor and miserable. Hitchens followed up with a scathing, book-length critique called 'The Missionary Position: Mother Teresa in Theory and Practice', which noted that Mother Teresa once wrote to Judge Lance Ito requesting leniency for Charles Keating, the biggest fraud and embezzler in American history, who was sentenced to 10 year imprisonment by a state court in Los Angeles in 1992. His Savings & Loans racket stole a total of $252 million, mainly from small and poor depositor. Earlier, in the 1980s, Keating had donated some $1,250,000 to Mother Teresa. During his state trial, she wrote a letter to presiding Judge Lance Ito, saying that she was not informed about his business but she knew him as a man who was generous toward the poor.

Hitchens further accused Mother Teresa of denying painkillers to her dying patients due to her personal belief that physical suffering was good for spiritual well being. The editor of the medical journal, The Lancet, said her staff made little effort to distinguish between the critically ill and those who could be cured. Such criticism hurt. But no one could question her startling, almost abnormal, compassion. Not many cradle the diseased and dying. 'The poor', she said, 'do not want your bread, they want your love; the naked do not want your clothes, they want human dignity.'

Mother Teresa received criticisms regarding handling of funds donated to her Order. When her work earned fame around the world, money poured in from individuals and corporate benefactors. Mother Teresa never worried about funding the many expanding activities of her order. 'The Lord sends it', she once said. 'We do his work; he provides the means.' Though millions of dollars donated to Teresa's charity work, unfortunately, most of that money sat unused in various bank accounts while the sisters had to beg for food from local merchants.

Mother Teresa also met with another set of criticism when she visited Albania in 1990. When she made a trip to Albania, she paid tribute to the late Enver Hoxha, the longtime proto-Stalinist boss of Albania, Mother Teresa's birthplace. Many Albanians were shocked when she embraced Hoxha's widow and her silence on human rights.

The Home for the Dying in Calcutta also attracted criticism. Unlike in modern hospices in the West, the dying at the mission homes, were not provided with pain-killing drugs. In November 1996 a German volunteer questioned one of Teresa's nuns. 'I have heard you don't give any medicines,' he said. The nun replied, 'This is not a treatment center. This is a place where the dying can die with dignity.'

Dr. Aroup Chatterjee, a Kolkata-born doctor settled in England, wrote a book "Mother Teresa: The Final Verdict" (2003), which dealt with her accounting policies, her politics, her relationship with Kolkata, views from within her charity homes, profiles of Kolkata's destitute based on extensive interviews and a comparison of her organisation's work with that of other religious and secular charities. His issue was not so much that she did not address suffering, but asserted that there was a 'stupendous discrepancy between her image and her work'. Though Chatterjee's book earned accolades in the West, his views did not go down well with the Catholic clergy in Kolkata associated with Mother Teresa and her Missionaries of Charity. While reviewing Chatterjee's book, journalist-writer Khushwant Singh observed that it was 'hard on facts, but weak on judgement'.

Apart from Christopher Hitchens and Dr. Aroup Chatterjee, the official critics of Mother Teresa, some other critics said that she was obsessed with poverty, that she lived off it, but made no move to remove it. Unshaken by such criticisms, Mother said, "You take care of their tomorrows, I take care of their todays."

A columnist in The Frontline magazine aptly wrote, 'Mother Teresa, then, had two personas. One was the ideologically retrogressive adherent to the views of the Papacy under John Paul II (in fact, the crystallisation of her own perceptions on these matters predate the present Papacy). The other was the trail-blazer who put Christian charity into action as no one else has done in the modern age. It is the second persona that the world will remember - Mother Teresa of the Poor.'

Though her philosophy on some issues met with criticism, her work did not undermine or topple her overall achievement. She will be remembered as Mother Teresa of the Poor for her selfless service with love and compassion.

7

PASSING ON THE CROWN

On several occasions, Mother Teresa was asked what would be the position of Missionaries of Charity after her. Once in an interview she was asked who would be her successor. She raised her finger and pointed towards heaven and said, "Let me go first. Just as God found me, He will find somebody else. The work is God's work and He will see to it." Mother Teresa never worried about her Order, as she believed that her work would be carried on even without her presence guided by Him.

After a decade of establishing her Order, Mother tried to pass on the leadership of Missionaries of Charity to someone else. According to the constitution of the Missionaries of Charity approved by the Holy Spirit, the 'Chapter General', which was made up of regional delegates who were elected from the various foundations of the Convent throughout the world have to meet every six years to elect its Superior General. The constitution also stated that the

Superior General could be elected for a second but not for the third time without the special permission of the Holy Spirit.

In 1961, the very first Chapter General made up of the Sister Superior and a deputy from each house met for the first time. Mother was elected, obviously, the Superior General. The Vatican allowed the two-term regulation in the case of Mother as she was the foundres of the Society.

In 1964, she was badly injured in a car accident in Darjeeling. She believed deeply in the relationship between the pains offered by God and creative growth. Thus, for her, accident was a mere chance to move towards God and achieve spiritual goals.

The second Chapter General took place in 1967 and Mother was again elected the Superior General. In 1973, again all the votes were for 'Mother', except her own vote. By 1985, during the Chapter General, Mother had health problems which really created obstacles in the path of her activities. Mother anxiously looked forward for a new Superior General in 1985 election. But the Sisters did not allow her step down and again re-elected Mother as the Superior General.

Despite her reduced activities and visits due to poor health condition and handing over responsibilities to the elected councilors, she shouldered the central burden of Missionaries of Charity.

Mother Teresa's health worsened in 1989 when she had a near fatal heart attack. Her condition worsened which caused great concern throughout the World. Messages of sympathy flowed from all over the world. She was fitted with a temporary, external pacemaker to control an irregular heartbeat. Finally, after more than a month of treatment, she recovered completely and doctors warned to stop her global-visits.

Following the nearly fatal heart attack, Mother Teresa announced her intention to retire. She said, 'God will find another person, more humble, more devoted, more obedient to him, and the society will go on.' On April 11, 1990, it was announced worldwide that Pope John Paul II had accepted the resignation of Mother Teresa as Superior General of the Missionaries of Charity, on the ground of her physical condition. A conclave of sisters was called to choose her successor. During a secret ballot of her sisters, Mother was re-elected with only one dissenting vote - her own. Mother, who was 80 years old by then, accepted her re-election as the will of God.

In December 1991, she underwent an angioplasty to clear the blocked coronary arteries after suffering from heart failure due to pneumonia. Her condition slowly improved. In May 1993, after returning from Antwerp, she fell on a wet floor in the bathroom in Rome and injured three ribs. Despite her injuries, she traveled as usual. In August 1993, she was again admitted to the All India Institute of Medical Sciences, in New Delhi, where she had gone to receive an award from the government of India for 'promoting peace and communal harmony'. Suddenly, she was taken ill shortly before the ceremony due to the congestion of lungs and breathlessness. She came close to death when doctors operated her closed heart vessel. Despite her ailing health, Mother Teresa ministered to wounds which needed healing, to souls which needed saving. She continued to feed the hungry, clothe the naked, shelter the homeless, comfort the sick and console the dying.

On 17 September 1993, Mother was once again fighting for her life as surgeons struggled to clear a blocked heart vessel. Pope John Paul II sent her a message saying, "The world needs you." When she was recouping, she was conscious of the work that was half-done. While staying at the hospital, on September 21, her spiritual director, Father Celeste Van Exem died in St. Xavier's College, Kolkata. Mother remained very close to him till the last. On his death, she said, 'He has gone straight to the home of God. He was very holy.'

After her close shave with death, Mother Teresa once said, "I went to heaven's gate but St. Peter told me, `Go back. There are no poor people here to be cared for.' So I came back to continue my work". Ivan Divas, who served for 5 years as the bishop of Albania until early 1997, equated her humor with her saintliness. He said that Mother had a sense of quiet humor, which was a sign of sanctity.

Ann Blaikie, who co-founded the Sick & Suffering Co-Workers, died peacefully of a pulmonary infection on January 14, 1996 at the age of seventy-nine.

On the midnight of March 31, 1996, Mother fell out of bed at the Mother House in Calcutta and broke her collarbone. In spite of being weak, she visited United States, Rome and Ireland in the month of June. Mother was asked to rest, as she was very weak. But, she simply said: "There will be plenty of time to rest in eternity. Here there is so much to do." She repeatedly rallied back from life-threatening respiratory problem in August 1996, with a determination some described as miraculous. But heart, lung, and other ailments caused her much pain, and forced her to stay in a wheelchair or bed most of the time.

In January, 1997, Archbishop Henry D'souza of Kolkata announced that Mother wanted to resign as Superior General of her Order as she was not in a position to continue due to ill health. He also informed that she had made it clear that there should not be any repetition of 1990 election where she had been re-elected despite her resignation. Delegates from around the world began meeting at the "Mother House" in Calcutta to elect a successor. The choice of the successor was proving to be difficult.

Finally, the announcement came on Thursday, March 13, 1997. Sister Nirmala, one of Mother Teresa's earliest disciples, was elected as the Superior General of Missionaries of Charity. Sister Nirmala, who was in charge of its Latin America network in the 1970s, returned to Calcutta in 1979 to head the order's contemplative wing. According to Archbishop Henry D' Souza, Sister Nirmala was elected 'almost unanimously' by 123 fellow Sisters from the order's far-flung centers. Most of the Order's sisters and brothers were South Asian, which also helped the candidacy of Sister Nirmala.

After her election, Sister Nirmala was asked whether she found herself the right person to accept the foundress's (Mother's) wonderful mantle (crown) or not; she replied, 'The Lord will make me fit for the job, if you pray for me.'

Sister Nirmala was a Hindu convert, from a Nepali family and a deeply spiritual, well-educated and a wise person. When Nirmala Joshi's parents put their daughter into a Catholic missionary school in the 1940s, their intention was for the girl to pick up some English and Arithmetic. What they hadn't expected was that their daughter would convert to Catholicism and dedicate her life to the poor. 'I was at the bus stand when I first felt Jesus was alive in my heart,' recalled Sister Nirmala in an interview with the Time Magazine.

After her bus-stop epiphany, she wrestled with her conscience for seven years before being baptized at the age of 24. The defining experience, she told TIME, was the Partition of 1947, when colonial India was bifurcated, Hindus and Muslims slaughtered each other by the tens of thousands, and millions of refugees were left homeless and dying. "There was so much killing," Nirmala said. "Everybody was just going mad. There was little compassion anywhere." She headed off to Calcutta, which was then packed with refugees from East Bengal. There, two Carmelite sisters directed her to Mother Teresa, who was spending her days tending to the poor and begging for funds to buy food and medicine for her mission. "It was inspiration at first sight," said Sister Nirmala. "Here was someone who could bring some compassion and a sense of destiny to people," she recalled about her first meeting with Mother Teresa. She joined the Missionaries of Charity on 24th May 1958.

Sweet-tempered and shy in public, Sister Nirmala, insisted that she was hardly a duplicate of her renowned predecessor. "I am not Mother Teresa, I'm Sister Nirmala," she told journalists at the order's Calcutta headquarters, where she was surrounded by cheering nuns. "Please don't call me Mother." Mother Teresa appeared beside her, obviously frail but smiling, and said, "I am very happy." Sister Nirmala then expressed doubts about her own ability to replace Mother Teresa. "Looking at myself, I am afraid," she said. "But looking at God and depending on the prayer and guidance of our Mother, I am sure I will be able to do what I have been chosen for. Please pray." She added: "I am in a dreamland."

After the election of her successor, Mother Teresa was asked if she would now retire, she replied: 'I still have a lot of work to do, and opening a branch in China is one of the works I hope to complete before I am gone.'

When Sister Nirmala took over the charge, the Missionaries of Charity had 3,500 sisters, ran 569 centers in 120 countries, aiding everyone from AIDS sufferers and lepers to orphans and earthquake victims. In Calcutta every year, the order fed half a million families, gave schooling to 20,000 children and provides medical care to 90,000 lepers.

Many related Sister Nirmala's compassion to that of Mother Teresa.'

Sister Agnes, Mother's first postulant died of cancer on April 9, 1997. In May 1997, Mother visited Rome and introduced her successor to him. She celebrated her eighty-seventh birthday in the 'Mother House.'

The death of Princess Diana in a car accident in Paris on 31st August 1997 moved the immensely frail Mother Teresa. They both shared compassion and a willingness to break through social walls. Mother Teresa always said, 'Diana is my daughter.' With utmost humility Diana said, "I am a very, very small Mother Teresa.' In June of 1997, Princess Diana visited Mother Teresa in New York City's South Bronx, where Mother Teresa was recuperating from an illness at one of her order's residences. The Princess came to meet Mother Teresa, to pay her respects, and to honor the work she herself was just beginning. They met and chatted about the work they loved for approximately an hour. Diana helped Mother Teresa rise from her wheelchair, and the two of them emerged from a private conversation holding hands, to be greeted by squealing children in the street. They were affectionate towards each other and put their faces close together. Mother Teresa clasped her palms together in the Indian gesture signifying both hello and good-bye. The princess got into her silver car, and that was the end of their first private visit, and unfortunately for the world, their last.

When Mother Teresa heard about Princess Diana's tragic death, in spite of her poor health condition, she appeared in the media and spoke of the Princess's love for the poor and promised that she would offer special prayers for Diana. According to news reports, this was Mother Teresa's last public statement.

DEATH

On the morning of September 5, 1997, Mother Teresa complained of chest pain and was examined by her personal physician Dr. Ashim Bardhan. But the pain persisted and, at 8.00 p.m. after a typically frugal dinner of bread and soup, "I cannot breathe", was all she said. An urgent summons was carried to Dr. Alfred Woodward, an American doctor attached to the Missionaries of Charity, who rushed to her bedside. Her head was resting in Sister Gertrude's hands and her eyes gazing at the picture of Christ – the Christ in agony as He lay dying, the crown of thorns embedded in his flesh, blood pouring down his left cheek, his eyes turned heavenwards. At about 9:30 p.m., she died – like she lived – quietly.

As news of her death spread, hundreds of grief-stricken followers of Mother Teresa in Calcutta gathered outside Mother House, the order's headquarters. The whole world plunged into deep sorrow on hearing the death of Mother Teresa, who was called the "Saint of the Gutters" for her work with the poor, destitute and dying.

Indian Prime Minister Inder Kumar Gujral mourned the death of Mother Teresa, saying the world had become poorer because of her loss. He said in a statement, 'Mother Teresa is no more with us. The world and especially India is poorer by her passing away. Her life was devoted to bringing love, peace and joy to people whom the world generally shuns.'

On the night she died and the next day, Mother Teresa's body was kept in the chapel at Mother House. Mother Teresa was laid under a glass case on a platform draped in the white and blue colors of her Missionaries of Charity Order, her hands folded across her chest. The Government of India announced that Mother Teresa would receive a State funeral. The honor of state rites was normally reserved for Prime Ministers and Presidents, although an exception also was made for Mahatma Gandhi. To order to allow time to the large number of mourners in Kolkata and elsewhere in India to reach to pay their last respects, as well as to give time to the large number of foreign delegations that had expressed their intention to attend the funeral, it was decided to hold the funeral eight days after her death, on 13 September 1997.

The outpouring of love and admiration for Mother Teresa came from the powerful and the humble of the world. World leaders from the Pope to Presidents joined the public and mourned the loss of a woman whose dedication to the poor and unwanted ignited compassion in many a cold heart. Pope John Paul II was 'deeply moved and pained' at her death.

Former President George Bush called her a wonderful woman. He said he and his wife, Barbara, 'greatly admired and respected her'. President Clinton called her one of the 'giants of our time' whose 'unconquerable faith' touched the lives of millions' in India, the United States and around the world. Mother Teresa 'personified a boldness of spirit and purity of soul,' former President Reagan and his wife Nancy said in a statement. French President, Jacques Chirac said, 'this evening there is in the world less love, less compassion, less light.'

Kofi Annon, head of the United Nations: (I offer my condolences) to all those who benefited from her humanitarian and development work, and to people around the world for whom Mother Teresa was a great symbol of compassion and hope. Russian President Boris Yeltsin: All of her life, this great lady was an example of commitment to humanitarian ideals as well as goodness, compassion, disinterest and faith. Former Pakistani premier and opposition leader Benazir Bhutto: The life of Mother Teresa teaches us a lesson that greatness lies in serving the humanity and to utilize our energies to build a better and fair society.

Religious leaders hailed her saying that she transcended national and sectarian differences by teaching universal values of compassion and justice.

Mother Teresa's death occurred on the heels of Princess Diana's funeral. The Princess was buried on 6th September 1997 with a rosary given to her by Mother Teresa.

On Sunday, 7 September, her body was taken to St. Thomas' Church, where hundreds of thousands of mourners filed past in final salutation.

Pope John Paul II paid tribute to Mother Teresa during the traditional Angelus prayers at Gastelgandolfo, his summer residence south of Rome, calling her fondly his "dear sister." He said that Mother Teresa 'was an eloquent example to all believers and non-believers. She was always full of inexhaustible internal energy, the energy of the love of Christ. The works which she accomplished speak for themselves and are a revelation to men of our time of the great significance of the values of life, which unfortunately are now getting lost'.

On 13 September 2007, her coffin was carried from St. Thomas church to Nehru Stadium on the gun carriage which was used to carry Mahatma Gandhi and Jawaharlal Nehru to their cremations. For six hours, thousands on Calcutta's streets and an international television audience of millions watched the final rites. The Indian Army conducted the proceedings with military precision. The Mass was preceded and followed by hymns in Bengali, Hindi and English, sung by the Missionaries of Charity Sisters. It ended with inter-faith readings by representatives of India's principal religions and faiths, who came together in a fitting crescendo of homage. Many world dignitaries were among the mourners. Mother Teresa's funeral service ended on Saturday with Indian army troops carrying her coffin from the Netaji stadium to Calcutta's Mother House. From the stadium the cortege was taken in a ceremonial procession through the streets of Calcutta on its predetermined route. Braving the light drizzle, people of all hues and shades, religions and castes, the wealthy and the poorest of the poor stood united in a moment of grief and waved her a final goodbye. The procession reached the burial site - Motherhouse - the final resting place for Mother Teresa, chosen by her Sisters.

Several nuns and priests watched as her coffin was lowered into a concrete tomb. The Indian Army fired their guns in final salute. Each one present put in a fistful of earth into the grave and gave a touching farewell to Mother Teresa. After the ceremonies, for which India had declared a day of national mourning, the normally crowded and vibrant streets of Calcutta were quiet and almost deserted.

Mother Teresa, who worked restlessly throughout her lifetime, was finally rested in a plain-cemented grave with a small marble tombstone that bore her name and an apt epitaph: **'Love one another as I have loved you'.**

8

BEATIFICATION

Once, during her visit to the United States 1982, she was asked about the popular conviction that she was already a saint. Her reply was: 'Please, let me die first!' Within days of her funeral, people began to petition the Vatican, Missionaries of Charity houses and churches everywhere to confer immediate canonization or sainthood on Mother Teresa. Sainthood means that Catholics around the world will be encouraged to venerate Mother Teresa for her heroic virtues. Mother Teresa, who dedicated her life to helping the poor and the outcast, was considered by many to be a living saint and attested her to be an ideal candidate for formal sainthood in the Roman Catholic Church. But years or decades may pass before the Roman Catholic Church can elevate her to sainthood. The church requires that two miracles attributed to the candidate's intercession with God be confirmed by the Vatican before canonization, except in the case of martyrdom. Miracles can come after the candidate's death, such as curing an ill believer or answering a supplicant's prayers. However, five years must pass after a death before the bishop can begin collecting proof of the "heroic virtue and reputation of holiness" of the person.

The process of canonization starts when the prelate — in the case of Mother Teresa the bishop of Calcutta — begins the cause, the candidate for sainthood receives the title 'Servant of God.' A 'postulator' is appointed to help gather information from people who knew the candidate, seeking evidence of holiness. In the case of Mother Teresa, the postulator would probably be a member of her Missionaries of Charity order. The evidence — usually amounting to many, many volumes — is sent under seal to the Vatican's Congregation for the Causes for Saints. A relator' is appointed. His job is to evaluate the evidence and make a recommendation in the form of a 'positio,' or position paper.

If the cause is begun more than 60 years after the death of the person, it is categorized as "ancient" and first goes to a historical commission in the Vatican congregation.

Recent causes that are based on witnesses go directly to a theological commission, which in turn passes the cause to a commission of cardinals for discussion.

If the investigation ends positively, a papal decree recognizing the person's "heroic virtues" is published and the person is granted the title of "venerable."

One miracle is required after a candidate's death for the cause to move on to Beatification. The miracle must be the result of a person praying to the candidate for intercession with God.

Miracles are usually the healing of medical conditions that doctors are at a loss to explain.

The candidate can then be beatified and declared a "blessed" of the Church. This allows a limited form of veneration, which in Mother Teresa's case would allow people in Calcutta as well as members of her order around the world to honor her. Another miracle is needed between the Beatification and Canonization, or the conferring of sainthood.

Many of the people who knew and worked with Mother Teresa are still alive. While this could speed up a cause because witnesses would be readily available to testify, the sheer volume of written, taped and filmed evidence of Mother Teresa's work could instead slow it down as all the proofs in any kind, shape or form must be seen, checked, controlled, judged, and evaluated.

In October 1997, Sister Nirmala met Pope John Paul II at the Vatican and apprised him of the growing demand for Mother Teresa's canonization. Archbishop Henry D'Souza of Kolkata wrote formally to the Congregation for the Causes of Saints, the department of the Vatican that deals with the complex issues of sainthood, for a first-ever dispensation from the rule of waiting for the mandatory five years after death, for the process of enquiry and investiation to begin. It normally takes decades – sometimes centuries – for the Vatican to complete the exhaustive inquiries it deems necessary to confirm without doubt purported mircalces of potential saints.

Cardinal Joseph Ratzinger, the Vatican's influential head of the Congregation of the Doctrine of Faith, said it was unlikely extra measures would be taken to hurry the process. 'Mother Teresa had a life so resplendent before the eyes of all, that I don't think it will be too long a process,' said Ratzinger in an interview with media persons.

Sister Nirmala and her people associated with the Missionaries of Charity believed that Mother Teresa will be canonized. However, according to the Vatican, any official canonization would have to wait because under the Vatican rules there has to be a five-year interval after a person's death. She said that Beatification – a primary step to sainthood – could come sooner.

Pope John Paul II, one of Mother Teresa's most ardent admirers, was a firm believer in promoting saints as models of virtue. Since assuming the papacy in 1978, John Paul had canonized 278 people and beatified 768. Both numbers exceed those of all other popes this century put together.

On 12 December 1998, Pope John Paul II, for the first time in the history of the Catholic Church granted a special dispensation from the rule of waiting. He took the unprecedented decision to speed up the process for Mother Teresa's beatification, citing overwhelming popular demand. The very idea of 'fast track sainthood' seemed a contradiction in terms in the offices of the Vatican's Congregation for the

Causes of Saints which had been collecting voluminous dossiers on holy men and women since the year 1588. There were arguments that Mother Teresa should not be given special privilege and controversy continued to surround her dealings with some of her benefactors. But in spite of the criticisms, it was expected that the Pope would beatify Mother Teresa soon.

The Beatification and Canaonization of Mother Teresa involved broadly two phases, the Diocesan Phase based in Kolkata and the Roman Phase at the Vatican. In March 1999, in accordance with the Vatican's rules, Sister Nirmala with the consent of the Archbishop of Kolkata, appointed Father Brian Kolodiejchuk, a Canadian Missionary of Charity priest, as the Diocesan Postulator, assisted by Sister Lynn Mascarenhas of Missionaries of Charity as Vice-Postulator. On 26 July 1999 the Archbishop formally opened the Cause of Beatification and Canonization of the Servant of God, Mother Teresa of Kolkata and called upon those with any substantial information concerning Mother Teresa to give evidence if they wished to. This included her critics as well. The team spent two and a half years in sifting through thousands of letters and documentary material received as well as supervising the recording of oral testimony in Kolkata.

On 15 August 2001, the Diocesan enquiry was officially concluded and the team produced 35,000 pages of testimony and documents bound in seventy-six volumes. The investigation team in Calcutta concluded that she showed the heroic qualities demanded for a saint. Hundreds of miracles were attributed to Mother Teresa, but most of them were termed as 'favours' and 'graces.' The only miracle that was eventually selected and went before a Special Enquiry Board was from the village of Dakshin Dinajpur in West Bengal. Monica Besra, a 32-year old woman, was suffering from abdominal pain. Even six months of medication and treatment, she was not cured. Later, she was diagnosed as suffering from TB meningitis and was brought to the house of the Missionaries of Charity at Patiram. The Sisters admitted her into the Tuberculosis Ward in the government hospital. However, Monica's health conditions did not improve even after continued medical attention. The Sisters, feeling that their efforts of the last few months had not cured, decided to perform a special prayer for her as she lay on her bed on the 5th September 1998 – the first death anniversary day of Mother Teresa. They placed on her stomach a small medallion which Mother had given to one of the Sisters and prayed over her. After a few hours after this prayer, Monica got up from her sleep feeling lighter with no pain. She and her husband believed that the miraculous intervention of Mother Teresa had cured her of tumour. However, this case had its own share of controversy. The doctors at the government hospital claimed that Monica was treated by them and had responded favourably to the treatment.

In January 2002, the report of Diocesan Enquiry in Kolkata was taken to the Vatican for the second phase of enquiry. The miracle in question was examined in a closed–door meeting between a commission of doctors and officials from the Catholic Church's Congregation for the Causes of

Saints. The doctors who examined the case said that they had no explanation for the cure. The Church officials declared the incident scientifically inexplicable. The case was finally cleared at the levels of cardinals and bishops attributing the miraculous cure to Mother Teresa's intercession and was sent to Pope John Paul II for his approval.

Meanwhile, in August 2002, Mother Teresa was voted as the 'greatest Indian' since the country's independence in 1947 in a survey conducted by 'Outlook' magazine.

The date of her beatification fell on 'Mission Sunday, closest to the 25th anniversary of the pontificate of the Pope and to the end of the year of the Rosary. Some Catholics considered this as a sign of how close Mother Teresa's cuase was to the pope's heart. During the three and a half year investigation into Mother Teresa cause, every nook and cranny of her life was studied for evidence that she was the great saint that the world had already believed her to be. Between November and December 2002, Zenit News Agency published in four installments a study of 'The Soul of Mother Teresa: Hidden Aspects of her Interior Life,' by the Postulator of Mother Teresa's cause, Father Brian Kolodiejchuk. In this study, which formed a part of her dossier sent to Rome from India, a new portrait of Mother Teresa's interior life emerges, drawn largely from letters she sent to her spiritual directors. She had wanted the letters to be destroyed, not intending to leave behind any record of her spiritual life ("I want the work to remain only His"), but they were preserved nonetheless.

According to Carol Zaleski, is a professor of religion at Smith College in Northampton, Massachusetts, wrote, 'Fr. Kolodiejchuk's study shows Mother Teresa as a classic Christian mystic whose inner life was burned through the fire of charity, and whose fidelity was tested and purified by an intense trial of faith, a true dark night of the soul. Fr. Kolodiejchuk sees Mother Teresa's life as unfolding in four phases:

Her childhood and youth, when from the time of her First Communion at age five and a half she felt her heart captivated by the love of Jesus and of neighbor, and discovered her call to join the missionary Sisters of Our Lady of Loreto. While it was difficult to leave her family, she found her time as a Loreto nun, teaching in the convent school in Calcutta, immensely rewarding. She was by all accounts a happy though not particularly brilliant nun (she is remembered, among other things, for having fumbled the candles at Benediction). The keynote of this period is youthful zeal and joy.

The Vow of 1942. At age thirty-two, at the end of her annual retreat, with the permission of her spiritual director, Mother Teresa made a vow to give herself utterly and unreservedly to Christ: "To give God anything that He may ask . . . not to refuse Him anything.'

The Call within a Call. On September 10, 1946, the day celebrated by the Missionaries of Charity as "Inspiration Day," Mother Teresa was traveling by train from Calcutta to a retreat house in Darjeeling. During this trip, the realization came to her that Jesus was calling her to serve him radically in the poorest of the poor. Only in private letters to her spiritual director, Fr. Celeste Van Exem, S.J., and (under Fr. Van Exem's cautious instruction) to Archbishop Ferdinand Périer, S.J., did she reveal that this call was more than just an inner prompting. Jesus appeared and spoke to her, in a series of interior locutions and visions. "Wouldst thou not help?" Jesus asked her. "How can I?" Mother Teresa responded, expressing her fear of incurring ridicule, loneliness, deprivation, and failure should she leave her happy life as a Loreto nun, exchange her habit for a rough sari, and take up the uncertain life Jesus was demanding of her. Repeatedly he asked her, "Wilt thou refuse? You have become my spouse for my love. You have come to India for me. The thirst you had for souls brought you so far. Are you afraid now to take one more step for your spouse, for me, for souls?" And again: "I want Indian nuns, Missionaries of Charity, who would be my fire of love amongst the poor, the sick, the dying, and the little children. . . ." The chief motivation for the Missionaries of Charity, as she would often say, was not to do social work, but to adore Christ in the littlest and weakest of his children, and to bring Christ the souls for which he thirsts.

The Dark Night: Throughout 1946 and 1947, Mother Teresa experienced a profound union with Christ. But soon after she left the convent and began her work among the destitute and dying on the street, the visions and locutions ceased, and she experienced a spiritual darkness that would remain with her until her death. It is hard to know what is more to be marveled at: that this twentieth-century commander of a worldwide apostolate and army of charity should have been a visionary contemplative at heart; or that she should have persisted in radiating invincible faith and love while suffering inwardly from the loss of spiritual consolation. In letters written during the 1950s and 1960s to Fr. Van Exem, Archbishop Périer, and to later spiritual directors, Fr. L. T. Picachy, S.J., and Fr. J. Neuner, S.J., she disclosed feelings of doubt, loneliness, and abandonment. God seemed absent, heaven empty, and bitterest of all, her own suffering seemed to count for nothing, ". . . just that terrible pain of loss, of God not wanting me, of God not being God, of God not really existing."

Mother Teresa is not the only modern saint to have undergone such a trial of faith; one thinks also of precursors like St. Paul of the Cross (1694-1775), founder of the Passionists, and St. Jane Frances de Chantal (1572-1641), foundress of the Visitandines, but above all of Mother Teresa's namesake, St. Thérèse of Lisieux (1873-1897), the French Carmelite famous for her "Little Way."

According to secret diaries and letters, which she told her spiritual director not to publish during her lifetime, Mother Teresa was haunted by religious doubt. Italian writer Saverio Gaeta wrote that 'Mother Teresa's faith in God was severely tested during one period of her life.'

Mother Teresa once wrote to a Jesuit priest confession that she has 'to keep smiling all the time'. They think that it is my faith, my hope and my love that is overwhelming me, and that my intimacy with God and union with His Will are filling my heart. If they only knew."

Rome theologian Manlio Asta commented, "Many saints of the Chruch have been mystics who suffered dark periods of doubt and torment about their faith. The fact that Mother Teresa also doubted cannot be an onstacle to her beatificaiton.

During the period of investigation process, in September 2001, the Archbishop Henry Sebastian D'Souza revealed that Mother Teresa underwent an exorcism in 1997 after a bout of insomnia was blamed on the devil. The exorcism took place in a hospital where Mother Teresa was admitted before her death on 5 September 1997. When doctors informed that they could not find a medical reason for her sleeplessness, the Archbishop feared that Mother Teresa might be possessed or under harassment from Satan. He wanted her to calm down and asked priest Rosariao Stroscio, in the name of the church, to perform an exorcism prayer on her, to which Mother Teresa also agreed. The Archbishop said that after the 'prayer of protection', she slept peacefully. He further said that the exorcism performed on Mother Teresa revealed Mother Teresa's human side and was a 'sign of closeness to God' and therefore, would not damage Mother Teresa's sanctity and the chances of achieving sainthood.

On 20 December 2002, Pope Johan Paul II signed the decree accepting the Monica's case as authentic miracle attributed to Mother Teresa. The Pope judged that the curing of Monica Besra who suffered from abdominal tumor, was the result of the supernatural intervention of Mother Teresa. The Pope's decision made it clear for Mother Teresa's beatification, a step closer to canonization or sainthood. The same day the Vatican announced that Pope John Paul II had set 19 October 2003 as the date for the beatification of Mother Teresa. No one ever had reached Beatification in such a short time as Mother Teresa. The Vatican normally adheres to strict church rules governing the making of saints. However, Pope John had already deviated from the church tradition of the customary five-year wait for the Diocesan Inquiry in to the life and virtue of Motehr Teresa putting the case into the fast track to sainthood.

Another deviation from the tradition of Roman Catholic Church was that the Vatican had decided not to exhume Mother Teresa's body. Usually, exhumation of the body is done before the ceremony of Beatification, which is a step to subsequent sainthood. According to Canon Law expert, Fr A C Jose, 'exhumation of the body was normally done to establish the identity of the person and also to ascertain the condition of the person's mortal remains.' But in Mother Teresa's case, this was not done, as, according to the Church sources, it was not mandatory to exhume of every candidate who are beatified.

As announced, Pope John Paul II beatified Mother Teresa during a ceremony on Sunday, the 19th October 2003 in St. Peter's Square at Vatican, Rome, bestowing one of his church's highest honours on the nun. John Paul, wheeled in an upholstered chair across the front steps of St. Peter's

Basilica toward an altar sheltered by a canopy, was pleased by the Vatican's jubilant crowd. The ceremony in Rome was the second huge gathering in a week in St Peter's Square which was also the scene of the Pope's 25th anniversary celebrations on 16 October 2003. The vast crowd outside the Vatican was a testament to Mother Teresa's huge popularity that cut across class, nationality and religion. Nuns from Mother Teresa's order, The Missionaries of Charity, came from almost 100 countries. Sister Nirmala presented the drops of blood in a reliquary to Pope John Paul II at the Beatification ceremony. The blood was drawn from the body of Mother Teresa during her hospitalization.

While addressing the crowd, the Pope said, "Brothers and sisters, even in our days God inspires new models of sainthood. Some impose themselves for their radicalness, like that offered by Mother Teresa of Calcutta, whom today we add to the ranks of the blessed. In her, we perceive the urgency to put oneself in a state of service, especially for the poorest and most forgotten, the last of the last." Her life is a testimony to the dignity and the privilege of humble service. She had chosen to be not just the least, but to be the servant of the least. As a mother to the poor, she bent down to those suffering various forms of poverty. Her greatness lies in her ability to give without counting the cost, to give `until it hurts'," Pope John Paul II said.

Nuns from the Missionaries of Charity wiped away tears and the crowd clapped when he pronounced her 'blessed'. "Her life of loving service to the poor has inspired many to follow the same path. Her witness and message are cherished by those of every religion as a sign that 'God still loves the world today," members of the Missionaries of Charity, the religious order she founded, said in a statement after Mother Teresa's beatification was announced. Since her death, they said, "people have sought her help and have experienced God's love for them through her prayers. Every day, pilgrims from India and around the world come to pray at her tomb, and many more follow her example of humble service of love to the most needy, beginning in their own families." A poster of her smiling, wrinkled face was unveiled to the crowd from the facade of the basilica.

Parkinson's disease had stiffened the Pope's facial muscles, and he was no longer able to stand or walk in public because of hip and knee ailments. He let aides read out his homily for him, including a tribute to Mother Teresa. In his homily, read by Bombay Cardinal Ivan Dias and others, John Paul said he was 'personally grateful to this courageous woman whom he had always felt at his side.'

Among those present at the Beatification ceremony were the Rome Mayor, Walter Veltroni, and the former Italian President, Oscar Luigi Scalfaro, as well as heads of state and government from several countries. Queen Fabiola of Belgium, royalty from Liechtenstein and Jordan, the presidents of Albania, Macedonia and Kosovo - in homage to Mother Teresa's roots in the Balkans and Muslim and Orthodox Christian delegations from Albania were also among the invitees for the ceremony. An Indian government delegation led by the Minister of State for Law and Justice, P.C. Thomas attended the beatification ceremony. After the ceremony in Rome, some 2,000 homeless men and women who eat and sleep in soup kitchens and shelters run by the Missionaries of Charity were given a special luncheon inside a Vatican hall.

In India, Mother's admirers and volunteers from different centres set up by the order, filed in by the scores to the Mother House, the headquarters of the Missionaries of Charity, in central Kolkata. Nuns and sisters congregated for prayers at a special morning mass, following which visitors were allowed to garland a life-size statue of the Mother in bronze and then pay their floral tributes at her marble tomb housed in the sanctum sanctorum. Hundreds of thousands of people including the inmates of leprosy centres and orphanages run by the Missionaries of Charity, watched the beatification ceremony live on television.

Following her beatification, Mother Teresa was now been called 'Blessed Teresa of Kolkata' - not just by Catholics but by people of all faiths across the globe. Another proven miracle is required for elevating Mother Teresa to sainthood.

PROCESS TO SAINTHOOD

If Mother Teresa of Calcutta had lived in earlier centuries, the Church might have gathered at her funeral to declare her a saint. That's the way things worked in ancient Christianity. Now achieving official sainthood is more complicated—and not without its own brand of politics and other human imperfections. But just as this "Saint of the Gutters" seemed above politics in her life, her utter and simple devotion to the poor will transcend bureaucratic obstacles between her and official sainthood.

Mother Teresa is already revered as a modern-day saint by Christians from all corners and denominations. Archbishop Henry D'Souza of Calcutta said that Mother Teresa's tomb "remains a shrine where people are praying and from which many are receiving grace and strength."

The delay in the process of canonization is that the Catholic Church thinks in centuries, not in years. It is good for the Church to test the enthusiasm of the day, to wait awhile, to discern whether one seen as a saint today will stand the test of time. As Archbishop D'Souza said, the Church "must be sure that someone who is declared to be a saint is truly such." The formal investigation will document details of Mother Teresa's life that may have gone unnoticed, and thus provide a wealth of information for generations to come.

D'Souza, though, a longtime friend of Mother Teresa's, expressed little doubt that "God would provide the miracles" to prove her cause. It was Teresa's single-mindedness, her simplicity and consistency that captured the world's imagination. One can only recall the beatitude of Jesus, "How happy are the pure of heart." That pureness of heart is a simple, single-minded commitment to the ways of God. We computer-dependent citizens of the 20th-century long for simplicity; Mother Teresa of Calcutta lived it.

9

A Symbol of Compassion

Mother Teresa always said that she was not trying to change the world, just make it more bearable and her work was only a drop in the ocean. She once said, "we offer a little comfort and a little love so that people can spend their last moments with dignity". Mother Teresa's charity and good deeds planted within others seeds of love from which love grows. She possessed a moral and spiritual beauty-reflected in her face, eyes and good deeds. Mother Teresa manifested the virtues of a genuinely liberated person: faith, hope, courage and charity.

Fr. Sebastian of Missionaries of Charity, while paying tribute to Mother Teresa, deeply analyzed what Mother Teresa learnt from her experience on 5 September 1946.

1) She learnt that the crucified Jesus of Nazareth is still hungry and thirsty for love of souls especially in the poorest of the poor irrespective of caste, colour, creed or nationality; and that she is being called to satiate and

satisfy the hunger and thirst of Jesus and of the poor through prayer, penance and whole-hearted free service to them.

2) She learnt that the needs of the person take precedence over any other consideration such as religion, colour or nationality. Her first question was not what religion he or she belonged to or what country he or she came from, but whether the person in question was in need of any help or not and what could I do for him or her to alleviate the pain. When I began working in the home for the dying in Kalighat (Calcutta) in the year 1967, there was a man close to death who was brought by the Calcutta Corporation Ambulance. Once inside with all the care and love, simple medicines and some food, he was able to regain his strength; as soon as he was a little better he would go out to the street again and then within a few days an ambulance would bring him back. This happened over ten to fifteen times within a couple of months' time. I used to get upset and even angry with him for this. One day when he was brought back, I told Mother Teresa, this man has been here over fifteen or more times; there is no meaning in taking him in again. In a couple of days' time he is going to go back to the street. Mother looked at me and said: "Listen, Brother Sebastian, does this man now need your help or not?". I said, yes. "Then do whatever you can to help him. The question is not how many times he has been to us but how can we help him now. Plus whatever we do to him we do it to Jesus. This

then is the point: although it was not the religion the person belonged to was her first consideration, every person she served was Jesus for her. She was always aware that whatever we do to the least of our brothers we do it to Jesus. And therefore:

3) She decided to make a fourth vow of whole hearted free service to the poorest of the poor in whom she loved and served Jesus.

4) Mother Teresa learnt that the same Jesus whom she loved and adored in the Bread of Life is the same Jesus whom she loved and served in the distressing disguise of the poorest of the poor. From the presence of Jesus in the Blessed Sacrament she went to the presence of Jesus in the poorest of the poor and vice versa. She used to say: "The more repugnant the poor is the more faith is required to help him".

5) Mother Teresa learnt that the work she was going to do was not social work but God's work. She repeatedly said: "Our work is not social work; it is God's work we are doing. We are not social workers, we are consecrated persons who are called to do God's work". This gives the clear answer to the question: what is going to happen now to the Missionaries of Charity? Because it is God's work and works of love it is going to continue, as long as we remain faithful to her Spirit and Charism.

6) Mother Teresa realized that she was not called to do extraordinary things, but ordinary things with extraordinary love. She repeatedly said: "It is not how

much we do that matters but how much love we put in our actions".

7) She learnt that not only she should hear the words of Jesus: "Come blessed of my Father..." but she should help all men of good will to hear it. She realized that she was called to build the bridge between the rich and the poor - the rich can find peace and joy in giving and sharing and the poor in receiving and returning. Both the rich and the poor give and receive mutually...

8) Mother Teresa learnt that it is in giving that we receive, in dying that we are born to eternal life. She realized that she was called to live the words of St. Paul: "It is more blessed to give than to receive" (Acts 20: 35).

9) Through Mother Teresa God opened the eyes of many to see their own poverty and misery and the poor thery are surrounded with and that they have to be "their brothers' keepers".

10) Mother Teresa made the world realize that there are two kinds of poverty: material and spiritual, both of which have positive and negative aspects. The spiritual poverty however is worse than the material poverty.

In conclusion we can say that although Mother Teresa died, had her most solemn funeral performed and her mortal remains have been laid in the tomb, her immortal spirit will continue to operate until the end of time and she from heaven will go on satiating the infinite thrirst of our Crucified Saviour for love of souls as she has become more powerful than ever.

"Each sigh, each look, each act of mine shall be an act of love divine, and everything I shall do, shall be, dear Lord, for love of you. Take this my heart and keep it true: a fountain sealed to all but you. What is there that I would not do today?" This was her prayer and her life. Let this be our prayer and our life as well. God bless you.'

In her 87 years, Blessed Mother Teresa's mission to help the poorest of the world was a pounding thirst she tried urgently to quench. With hands gnarled by time and a face weathered by age, Mother Teresa braved the polluted and overcrowded streets of India and beyond, embracing people whom many feared to touch, advocating for the world's most forgotten citizens. A true visionary, Mother Teresa saw past the wounds of lepers and comforted the sick as they wrestled with death. Simply, no person was beyond her capacity for love and assistance. Edging just past five feet in height, Mother Teresa was not a physically imposing figure. Yet her arms were long enough to embrace the thousands she saw as her own children.

Though Mother Teresa took a vow of poverty, died with few personal possessions, worked without pay, and did not seek publicity or promotion; she could easily be regarded as having become of the of the most famous people on the Earth, one of the richest in resources to accomplish whatever she chose to do, and one of the most respected and powerful people in the eyes of the rich and famous and powerful people who honored her, in her life and at her death. She was a living example of the Power of Love. However, she sought neither praise nor reward, though she earned both. Unimpressed with her own celebrity, Mother Teresa was single-minded in her pursuit to help the less fortunate. In their tattered faces, she saw the image of God. "I see God in every human being," she once said. "When I wash the leper's wounds, I feel I am nursing the Lord himself. Is it not a beautiful experience?"

When Mother Teresa died in September of 1997, the defeated of this world lost their greatest champion. The legacy of her work, however, is still with us.

Mother Teresa's life was a textbook of lessons we'd all be wise to study. In our lives, we should look to her as the model of patience and goodwill. Her ability to see the beauty in each person and the commonalities that bind the human race are gifts that we should attain.

Yet in our modern society, much is judged solely on what the eyes can show us. Mother Teresa looked at the world and its people with the eyes of her soul. She reminded us, in word and in action, that each of us is part of a whole and that all life is to be honored and protected.

In her life, Mother Teresa showed us a nobler way to look at our neighbors, both nationally and internationally. In her death, it should be our task to put those examples to use. Her tireless love of all people, from every culture, should be the standard by which we live.

To this blessed woman, no person in need of help was turned away, and anyone with an able body and a willing heart could join her family of workers. In her eyes, we were all children of God—the crippled, the healthy, the weak and the strong. In the sores of the lepers, she saw the wounds of Christ; in the hearts of the workers, she saw salvation. To those who felt called to such work, regardless of their nationality, religion or worldview, Mother Teresa—the "Saint of the Gutters"—took them each by the hand and seemed to say, with unwavering hope, "Come with me."

She was "Mother" to her nuns, and to millions of people around the world. She was the kind of loving mother we always wanted, or wanted to be. We miss our Mother Teresa, as we would miss our own mother. But like a mother who raises her children to take care of themselves, Mother Teresa trained thousands of devoted followers who will carry on with her great work. And we can carry on with her lessons in Love, by remembering how she showed us that a life of loving service to our fellow man is a life worth living, and a life that was rewarded with love and longevity, even with fame and good fortune.

The Spirit of Mother Teresa lives on in her good work carried on by the Missionaries of Charity she established. Her loving Spirit lives on in the love she inspired in us. Her humble but beautiful spirit lives on in the lesson she never tired of teaching through her enduring example of concern and care for others: we must love one another. The world will always remember Mother Teresa as a true 'Symbol of Compassion'.

Appendix-I

QUOTES OF MOTHER TERESA

Smiles

"Peace begins with a smile."

"Sometimes it is harder for us to smile at those who live with us, the immediate members of our families, than it is to smile at those who are not so close to us. Let us never forget: love begins at home."

"I will never understand all the good that a simple smile can accomplish."

"To smile at someone who is sad; to visit, even for a little while, someone who is lonely; to give someone shelter from the rain with our umbrella; to read something for someone who is blind; these and others can be small things, very small things, but they are appropriate to give our love of God concrete expression to the poor."

Family

"The woman is the heart of the home. Let us pray that we women realize the reason of our existence: to love and be loved and through this love become instruments of peace in the world."

"The most natural thing is the family life. What keeps the family together, what nourishes the life of the family together, is that surrender to each other; is that obedience; is that accepting of each other"

"We should teach our children to love one another at home. They can learn this only from their father and mother, when they see the parents' love for each other."

"To parents: It is very important that children learn from their fathers and mothers how to love one another—not in the school, not from the teacher, but from you. It is very important that you share with your children the joy of that smile. There will be misunderstandings; every family has its cross, its suffering. Always be the first to forgive with a smile. Be cheerful, be happy."

"Today we see more and more that all the suffering in the world has started from the home. Today we have no time even to look at each other, to talk to each other, to enjoy each other, and still less to be what our children expect from us, what the husband expects from the wife, what the wife expects from the husband. And so more and more we are out of our homes and less and less in touch with each other."

"Maybe in our own family we have somebody who is feeling lonely, who is feeling sick, who is feeling worried. Are we there? Let us know the poor in our own families first. We have old people: they are put in institutions and they are never visited; with less and less time even to smile at each other, with less and less time to be together. Love begins at home, if we can only make our own homes temples of love."

"I think of you and your families and pray for each one of you: 'Lord, keep them faithful to each other in Your love. Let nothing, nobody separate them from Your love and love for each other. Let the child, the gift of Yourself to every family, be the bond of love, unity, joy, and peace. Amen"

Life & Death

"In my heart, I carry the last glances of the dying. I do all I can so that they feel loved at that most important moment when a seemingly useless existence can be redeemed."

"The fact of death should not sadden us. The only thing that should sadden us is to know that we are not saints."

"At the moment of death, we will not be judged according to the number of good deeds we have done or by the diplomas we have received. We will be judged according to the love we have put into our work."

Love

"In your life, in mine, in the life of each of us, God has made us for bigger things. He has created us to love and to be loved, so that we walk toward our heavenly home. As we carry Jesus in the world, we will be prepared to return eagerly to our Father's house when the day arrives for us to be called home"

"The important thing is not how much we accomplish, but how much love we put into our deeds every day. That is the measure of our love for God."

"Love is a fruit, in season at all times and within the reach of every hand. Anyone may gather it and no limit is set. Everyone can reach this love through meditation, the spirit of prayer, and sacrifice."

"How do we love? Not in big things, but in small things with great love. There is so much love in us all. We must not be afraid to show our love."

"My sisters and I always greet the Lord and one another each morning at 4:30 a.m. with the words: 'Let us bless the Lord Thanks be to God.' Let us always greet each other with a smile—for a smile is the beginning of love."

"Love begins by taking care of the closest ones—the ones at home. Let us ask ourselves if we are aware that maybe our husband, our wife, our children, or our parents live isolated from others, do not feel loved enough, even though they may live with us. Do we realize this? Where are the old people today? They are in nursing homes (if there are any). Why? Because they are not wanted, because they are too much trouble, because....."

"Love is, just like Christ himself showed with his death, the greatest gift."

"All sicknesses have cures. The only one that cannot be cured is the sickness of feeling unloved. I invite all those who appreciate our work to look around them and be willing to love those who have no love and to offer them their services. Are we not, by definition, messengers of love?"

"Let us not love by words alone, but let us love until it hurts. It cost Jesus to love us. He even died for us. Now it is our turn to love one another as Jesus loved us. You must not be afraid to say "yes" to Jesus, because there is no greater love than his love and no greater joy than his joy."

"God pays attention to our love. Not one of us is indispensable. God has the means to do all things and to do away with the work of the most capable human being. We can work until we drop. We can work excessively. If what we do is not connected to love, however, our work is useless in God's eyes."

Loneliness

"There are many kinds of poverty. Even in countries where the economic situation seems to be a good one, there are expressions of poverty hidden in a deep place, such as the tremendous loneliness of people who have been abandoned and who are suffering."

"Everywhere there exists loneliness, the same deep need to be loved and cared for. Right in your midst there are those who suffer because they do not feel wanted or loved. They experience the anguish of having no one to call their own. This is real poverty without a doubt. We need to want to be someone for those who need us."

"As far as I am concerned, the greatest suffering is to feel alone, unwanted, unloved. The greatest suffering is also having no one, forgetting what an intimate, truly human relationship is, not knowing what it means to be loved, not having a family or friends."

"Homelessness is not only of bricks but homelessness comes from that terrible loneliness that the unwanted, the unloved know along their way. Are we there? Do we know them? Do we see them?"

The Poor

"None of us, I am sure, knows what is the pain of hunger, but one day I learned it from a little child. I found the child in the street and I saw in her face that terrible hunger that I have seen in many eyes. Without questioning her, I gave her a piece of bread, and then I saw that the little child was eating the bread crumb by crumb. And I said to her: 'Eat the bread.' And that little one looked at me and said; 'I am afraid because when the bread is finished, I will be hungry again.' "

"Jesus is the one we take care of, visit, clothe, feed, and comfort every time we do this to the poorest of the poor, to the sick, to the dying, to the lepers, and to the ones who suffer from AIDS."

"When a poor person dies of hunger, it has not happened because God did not take care of him or her. It has happened because neither you nor I wanted to give that person what he or she needed. We have refused to be instruments of love in the hands of God to give the poor a piece of bread, to offer them a dress with which to ward off the cold. It has happened because we did not recognize Christ when, once more, he appeared under the guise of pain, identified with a man numb from the cold, dying of hunger, when he came in a lonely human being, in a lost child in search of a home."

"The poor call to us. We have to be aware of them in order to love them. We have to ask ourselves if we know the truth. Do we know the poor in our own homes?"

"Sometimes people can hunger for more than bread. It is possible that our children, our husband, our wife, do not hunger for bread, do not need clothes, do not lack a house. But are we equally sure that none of them feels alone, abandoned, neglected, needing some affection? That, too, is poverty."

"I will never tire of repeating this: what the poor need the most is not pity but love. They need to feel respect for their human dignity, which is neither less nor different from the dignity of any other human being."

"The greatest injustice we have done to our poor people is that we think they are good for nothing; we have forgotten to treat them with respect, with dignity as a child of God. People have forgotten what the human touch is, what it is to smile, for somebody to smile at them, somebody to recognize them, somebody to wish them well. The terrible thing is to be unwanted."

"I repeat that the poor, the sufferers from leprosy, the rejected, the alcoholics, whom we serve, are beautiful people. Many of them have wonderful personalities. The experience which we have by serving them, we must pass on to people who have not had that wonderful experience."

"I was asked why I did not give a rod with which to fish, in the hands of the poor, rather than give the fish itself as this makes them remain poor. So I told them: The people whom we pick up are not able to stand with a rod. So today I will give them fish and when they are able to stand, then I shall send them to you and you can give them the rod. That is your job. Let me do my work today."

Prayer

"Everything starts with prayer. Love to pray—feel the need to pray often during the day and take the trouble to pray. If you want to pray better, you must pray more. The more you pray, the easier it becomes. Perfect prayer does not consist of many words but in the fervor of the desire which raises the heart to Jesus."

"The fruit of prayer is a clean heart and a clean heart is free to love. The fruit of love is Peace—Unity—Joy."

"Silence is the root of our union with God and with one another. In silence we are filled with the energy of God Himself that makes us do all things in joy. The more we receive in silent prayer, the more we can give in our active life."

"Let us all pray especially that people shall be brothers and sisters in the world and will understand this prayer. We can each think about it separately and examine our conscience. And let each of us ,before we pass the prayer on to somebody else, put this prayer into life: "Lead me from death to life, from falsehood to truth; Lead me from despair to hope, from fear to trust; Lead me from hate to love, from war to peace; Let peace fill our heart, our world, our universe."

"Today, more than ever, we need to pray....for the light to know the will of God.....for the love to accept the will of God....for the way to do the will of God."

"Do I need to pray? Do I want to pray? Remember wherever you may be—Mother Teresa's prayer, love and blessing will always be with you. God bless you."

"The world today is hungry not only for bread....but hungry for love; hungry to be wanted.. to be loved."

"The fruit of silence is prayer. The fruit of prayer is faith. The fruit of faith is love. The fruit of love is service. The fruit of service is peace."

"I see God in every human being. When I wash the leper's wounds, I feel I am nursing the Lord himself. Is it not a beautiful experience?"

"When a poor person dies of hunger, it has not happened because God did not take care of him or her. It has happened because neither you nor I wanted to give that person what he or she wanted."

"I have never seen war before, but I have seen famine and death. I was asking (myself), 'What do they feel when they do this?' I don't understand it. They are all children of God. Why do they do it? I don't understand."

"I realized that I had the call to take care of the sick and the dying, the hungry, the naked, the homeless - to be God's Love in action to the poorest of the poor. That was the beginning of the Missionaries of Charity."

"A nation that destroys the life of an unborn child, who has been created for living and loving, who has been created in the image of God, is in a tremendous poverty."

"When He was dying on the Cross, Jesus said, 'I thirst'. Jesus is thirsting for our love, and this is the thirst of everyone, poor or rich alike. We all thirst for the love of others, that they will go out of their way to avoid harming us and to do good to us. This is the meaning of truest love, to give until it hurts."

"Keep the joy of loving God in your heart and share this joy with all you meet, especially your family. Be holy—let us pray."

"There is no greater sickness in the world today than the lack of love."

"We can do no great things; only small things with great love."

"God loves a cheerful giver. She or he gives best who gives with a smile."

"The hunger for love is much more difficult to remove than the hunger for bread."

"Kind words can be short and easy to speak, but their echoes are truly endless."

"We need to find God, and God cannot be found in noise and restlessness. God is the friend of silence. See how nature—trees and flowers and grass—grow in silence. See the stars, the moon, and the sun, how they move in silence. The more we receive in silent prayer, the more we can give in our active life."

"God made the world rich enough to feed and clothe all human beings."

"The other day I dreamed that I was at the gates of heaven. And St. Peter said, 'Go back to Earth, there are no slums up here.' "

"Pride destroys everything. To imitate Jesus is the key to be meek and humble in heart."

"There is only one God and He is God to all; therefore it is important that everyone is seen as equal before God. I've always said we should help a Hindu become a better Hindu, a Muslim become a better Muslim, a Catholic become a better Catholic."

"People who love each other fully and truly are the happiest people in the world. They may have little, they may have nothing, but they are happy people. Everything depends on how we love one another."

"When I was crossing into Gaza, I was asked at the checkpost whether I was carrying any weapons. I replied: Oh yes, my prayer books."

"If you have a sick or lonely person at home, be there. Maybe just to hold a hand, maybe just to give a smile, that is the greatest, the most beautiful work."

"Prayer gives us a pure heart and a pure heart can do much."

"Keep your heart pure. A pure heart is necessary to see God in each other. If you see God in each other, there is love for each other, then there is peace."

"The poor do not need our sympathy and our pity. The poor need our love and compassion."

"I don't know what God is doing. He knows. We do not understand, but of one thing I'm sure, He doesn't make a mistake."

"God has created us to love and to be loved, and this is the beginning of prayer—to know that he loves me, that I have been created for greater things."

"The joy of Jesus will be my strength—it will be in my heart. Every person I meet will see it in my work, my walk, my prayer—in everything."

"Keep the light of Christ always shining in your hearts. Only He is the Way to be trodden. He is the Truth we must speak out. He is the Love we must love."

"Faith in action is love, and love in action is service. By transforming that faith into living acts of love, we put ourselves in contact with God Himself, with Jesus our Lord."

"Christ is hidden under the suffering appearance of anyone who is hungry, naked, homeless, or dying."

"People are hungry for God. Do you see that? Quite often we look but do not see. We are all passing through this world. We need to open our eyes and see."

"We must convert our love for Christ into deeds. We must express Christian love in concrete, living ways.

"Let us bring love and compassion to win the world, to bring the world the gospel of Christ. Let us all bring the good news that God loves the world!"

"You who have received so much love, share it with others. Love others the way that God has loved you, with tenderness."

"Communion with Christ gives us our strength, our joy, and our love."

"All of us must be saints in this world. Holiness is a duty for you and me. So let's be saints and so give glory to the Father."

"My prayer for you is that you come to understand and have the courage to answer Jesus' call to you with the simple word 'yes'."

"Love does not measure; it just gives."

The above quotes were taken from "Mother Teresa: In My Own Words"/by Mother Teresa/compiled by Jose Luis Gonzalez-Balado/Gramercy Books, Random House Publishing, Inc./1996; and from "Mother Teresa: The Joy In Loving"/by Mother Teresa/compiled by Jaya Chaliha and Edward Le Joly/Viking Penguin/1996.

Appendix-II

TIME LINE

Mother's life in chronological order

Aug 26,1910	Agnes Gonxha Beiaxhiu born, in Skopje in Macedonia, the youngest of three children of an Albanian family.
1928	Leaves home for Dublin, Ireland, to become a Loretto nun. She takes the name sister Teresa
1929	Arrives in Calcutta, India and joins St Mary's High school to teach.
May 24, 1937	Takes final vows as a nun in Darjeeling.
1947	Most important journey of her life to Darjeeling where she receives a call from Jesus to serve him among the poorest of poor and to live with them.
1948	Opens first slum school in Calcutta.
1950	Missionaries of Charity established.

1952	Opens Nirmal Hriday, or Pure heart, a home for dying
1962	Receives the Padmashri award for distinguished service - her first award for her humanitarian work.
1971	Pope John Paul VI awards Mother peace prize.
1979	Gets the Nobel Peace Prize.
1980	Awarded India's highest civilian honour Bharat Ratna.
1983	Has a heart attack while in Rome visiting Pope John Paul II.
1983	Queen Elizabeth II awards Order of Merit in New Delhi.
1985	Gets Medal of Freedom, the highest US civilian award.
1986	Narrow escape in an air crash in Tanzania.
1989	Suffers second heart attack; doctors implant pacemaker.
1990	Wants to relinquish charge of Missionaries of Charity on account of poor health. But she is re-elected with only one dissenting vote - her own.
1991	Suffers pneumonia in Mexico, and undergoes heart surgery in the United States.
1993	Breaks three ribs in fall in Rome.

1993	Another surgery in Calcutta to clear a blocked heart vessel.
1996	Fractures her left collar bone and is hospitalised.
Aug 22, 1996	Suffers heart failure, admitted to Calcutta's Woodlands Nursing Home.
Sep 16, 1996	Injures head in fall while getting out of bed; doctors detect spot on brain.
Nov 16, 1996	Granted honorary American citizenship.
Nov 22,1996	Taken to Woodlands Nursing Home with irregular heartbeat.
Nov 29, 1996	Undergoes angioplasty surgery to remove two blockages in major coronary arteries.
March 13, 1997	Sister Nirmala elected to succeed Mother Teresa as leader of Missionaries of Charity.
May 16, 1997	Arrives in Italy for a two-month tour and is given oxygen at Rome airport because of weariness.
June 18,1997	Meets Princess Diana for fourth time at Missionaries of Charity residence in New York.
Sept 5, 1997	Mother dies following a heart attack at her religious order's headquarters in Calcutta
1999	Beatification Process begins
September	Vatican approves beatification
October 19, 2003	Beatification

Appendix-III

LECTURE AT U.S. BREAKFAST PRAYER

Whatever You Did Unto One of the Least, You Did Unto Me

by Mother Teresa of Calcutta

From the National Prayer Breakfast, Washington, D.C., February, 1994

"On the last day, Jesus will say to those on His right hand, 'Come enter the Kingdom. For I was hungry and you gave me food, I was thirsty and you gave me drink, I was sick and you visited me.' Then Jesus will turn to those on His left hand and say, 'Depart from me because I was hungry and you did not feed me, I was thirsty and you did not give me to drink, I was sick and you did not visit me.' These will ask Him, 'When did we see You hungry, or thirsty or sick and did not come to Your help?'. And Jesus will answer then, 'Whatever you neglected to do unto one of the least of these, you neglected to do unto Me!'

"As we have gathered here to pray together, I think it will be beautiful if we begin with a prayer that expresses very well what Jesus wants us to do for the least. St. Francis of Assisi understood very well these words of Jesus and His life is very well expressed by a prayer. And this prayer, which we say every day after Holy Communion, always surprises me very much, because it is very fitting for each one of us. And I always wonder whether 800 years ago when St. Francis lived, they had the same difficulties that we have today. I think that some of you already have this prayer of peace - so we will pray it together.

"Let us thank God for the Opportunity He has given us today to have come here to pray together. We have come here especially to pray for Peace, Joy, and Love. We are reminded that Jesus came to bring the good news to the poor. He had told us what is that good news when He said: 'My Peace I leave with you, My Peace I give unto you.' He came not to give the peace of the world which is only that we don't bother each other. He came to give the Peace of heart which comes from loving - from doing good to others.

"And God loved the world so much that He gave His Son - it was a giving. God gave His Son to the Virgin Mary, and what did she do with Him? As soon as Jesus came into Mary's life, immediately she went in haste to give that good news. And as she came into the house of her cousin, Elizabeth, Scripture tells us that the unborn child - the child in the womb of Elizabeth - leapt with joy. While still in the womb of Mary - Jesus brought Peace to John the Baptist who leapt for joy in the womb of Elizabeth.

"And as if that were not enough, as if it were not enough that God the Son should become one of us and bring Peace and Joy while still in the womb of Mary, Jesus also died on the Cross to show that greater Love. He died for you and for me, and for that leper and for that man dying of hunger and that naked person lying in the street, not only of Calcutta, but of Africa, and everywhere. Our Sisters serve these poor people in 105 countries throughout the world. Jesus insisted that we love one another as He loves each one of us. Jesus gave His Life to love us and He tells us that we also have to give whatever it takes to do good to one another. And in the Gospel Jesus says very clearly: 'Love as I have loved you.'

"Jesus died on the Cross because that is what it took for Him to do good to us - to save us from our selfishness in sin. He gave up everything to do the Father's Will - to show us that we too must be willing to give up everything to do God's Will - to love one another as He loves each of us. That is why we too must give to each other *until it hurts.*

"It is not enough for us to say: 'I love God', but I also have to love my neighbor. St. John says that you are a liar if you say you love God and you don't love your neighbor. How can you love God whom you do not see, if you do not love your neighbor whom you see, whom you touch, with whom you live? And so it is very important for us to realize that love, to be true, has to hurt. I must be willing to give whatever it takes not to harm other people and, in fact, to do good to them. This requires that I be willing *to give until it hurts.*

Otherwise, there is no true love in me and I bring injustice, not peace, to those around me.

"It hurt Jesus to love us. We have been created in His Image for greater things, to love and to be loved. We just 'put on Christ' as Scripture tells us. And so, we have been created to love as He loves us. Jesus makes Himself the hungry one, the naked one, the homeless one, the unwanted one, and He says, "You did it unto Me." On the last day He will say to those on His right, 'Whatever you did to the least of these, you did to Me', and He will also say to those on His left, 'Whatever you neglected to do for the least of these, you neglected to do it for Me'.

"When He was dying on the Cross, Jesus said, 'I thirst'. Jesus is thirsting for our love, and this is the thirst of everyone, poor or rich alike. We all thirst for the love of others, that they will go out of their way to avoid harming us and to do good to us. This is the meaning of truest love, *to give until it hurts.*

"I can never forget the experience I had in visiting a home where they kept all these old parents of sons and daughters who had just put them into an institution and forgotten them - maybe. I saw that in that home these old people had everything - good food, comfortable place, television, everything, but everyone was looking toward the door. And I did not see a single one with a smile on the face. I turned to Sister and I asked: 'Why do these people, who have every comfort here, why are they all looking toward the door? Why are they not smiling?'

"I am so used to seeing the smiles on our people, even the dying ones smile. And Sister said: 'This is the way it is nearly every day. They are expecting, they are hoping that a son or daughter will come to visit them. They are hurt because they are forgotten.' And see, this neglect to love brings spiritual poverty. Maybe in our own family we have somebody who is feeling lonely, who is feeling sick, who is feeling worried. Are we there? Are we willing *to give until it hurts* in order to be with our families, or do we put our own interests first? These are the questions we must ask ourselves, especially as we begin this year of the family. We must remember that love begins at home and we must also remember that the future of humanity passes through the family."

Appendix-IV

Homily of His Holiness John Paul II

WORLD MISSION SUNDAY

Sunday, 19 October 2003

1. *"Whoever would be first among you must be slave of all"* (Mk10: 44). Jesus' words to his disciples that have just rung out in this Square show us the way to evangelical "greatness". It is the way walked by Christ himself that took him to the Cross: a journey of love and service that overturns all human logic. *To be the servant of all!*

Mother Teresa of Calcutta, Foundress of the Missionaries of Charity whom today I have the joy of adding to the Roll of the Blesseds, allowed this logic to guide her. I am personally grateful to this courageous woman whom I have always felt beside me. Mother Teresa, *an icon of the Good Samaritan,* went everywhere to serve Christ in the poorest of the poor. Not even conflict and war could stand in her way.

Every now and then she would come and tell me about her experiences in her service to the Gospel values. I remember, for example, her pro-life and anti-abortion interventions, even when she was awarded the Nobel Prize for peace (Oslo, 10 December 1979). She often used to say: "If you hear of some woman who does not want to keep her child and wants to have an abortion, try to persuade her to bring him to me. I will love that child, seeing in him the sign of God's love".

2. Is it not significant that her beatification is taking place on the very day on which the Church celebrates *World Mission Sunday?* With the witness of her life, Mother Teresa reminds everyone that *the evangelizing mission of the Church passes through charity,* nourished by prayer and listening to God's word. Emblematic of this missionary style is the image that shows the new Blessed clasping a child's hand in one hand while moving her Rosary beads with the other.

Contemplation and action, evangelization and human promotion: Mother Teresa proclaimed the Gospel living her life *as a total gift to the poor* but, at the same time, *steeped in prayer.*

3. *Whoever wants to be great among you must be your servant*" (Mk 10: 43). With particular emotion we remember today Mother Teresa, a great servant of the poor, of the Church and of the whole world. Her life is a testimony to the dignity and the privilege of humble

service. She had chosen to be not just *the least* but to be *the servant of the least.* As a real mother to the poor, she bent down to those suffering various forms of poverty. Her greatness lies in her ability to give without counting the cost, to give "until it hurts". Her life was a radical living and a bold proclamation of the Gospel.

The cry of Jesus on the Cross, *"I thirst"* (Jn 19: 28), expressing the depth of God's longing for man, penetrated Mother Teresa's soul and found fertile soil in her heart. *Satiating Jesus' thirst for love and for souls* in union with Mary, the Mother of Jesus, had become the sole aim of Mother Teresa's existence and the inner force that drew her out of herself and made her "run in haste" across the globe to labour for the salvation and the sanctification of the poorest of the poor.

4. *"As you did to one of the least of these my brethren, you did it to me"* (Mt 25: 40). This Gospel passage, so crucial in understanding Mother Teresa's service to the poor, was the basis of her faith-filled conviction that *in touching the broken bodies of the poor she was touching the body of Christ.* It was to Jesus himself, hidden under the distressing disguise of the poorest of the poor, that her service was directed. Mother Teresa highlights the deepest meaning of service - an act of love done to the hungry, thirsty, strangers, naked, sick, prisoners (cf. Mt 25: 34-36) is done to Jesus himself.

Recognizing him, she ministered to him with wholehearted devotion, expressing the delicacy of her spousal love. Thus, in total gift of herself to God and neighbour, Mother Teresa found her greatest fulfilment and *lived the noblest qualities of her femininity.* She wanted to be a sign of "God's love, God's presence and God's compassion", and so remind all of the value and dignity of each of God's children, "created to love and be loved". Thus was Mother Teresa "bringing souls to God and God to souls" and satiating Christ's thirst, especially for those most in need, those whose vision of God had been dimmed by suffering and pain.

5. *"The Son of man also came... to give his life as a ransom for many"* (Mk 10: 45). Mother Teresa shared in the Passion of the crucified Christ in a special way during long years of "inner darkness". For her that was a test, at times an agonizing one, which she accepted as a rare "gift and privilege".

   In the darkest hours she clung even more tenaciously to prayer before the Blessed Sacrament. This harsh spiritual trial led her to *identify herself more and more closely with those whom she served each day,* feeling their pain and, at times, even their rejection. She was fond of repeating that *the greatest poverty is to be unwanted,* to have no one to take care of you.

6. *"Lord, let your mercy be on us, as we place our trust in you".* How often, like the Psalmist, did Mother Teresa call on her Lord in times of inner desolation: "In you, in you I hope, my God!"

   Let us praise the Lord for this *diminutive woman in love with God,* a humble Gospel messenger and a tireless benefactor of humanity. In her we honour one of the most important figures of our time. Let us welcome her message and follow her example.

Virgin Mary, Queen of all the Saints, help us to be gentle and humble of heart like this fearless messenger of Love. Help us to serve every person we meet with joy and a smile. Help us to be missionaries of Christ, our peace and our hope. Amen!

http://www.vatican.va/holy_father/john_paul_ii/homilies/2003/documents/hf_jp-ii_hom_20031019_mother-theresa_en.html

Address of John Paul II to the Pilgrims who had come to Rome for the Beatification of Mother Teresa

Monday, 20 October 2003

Venerable Brothers in the Episcopate,
Dear Men and Women Missionaries of Charity,
Dear Brothers and Sisters,

1. I cordially greet you and joyfully join you in thanking God for the beatification of Mother Teresa of Calcutta. I was bound to her by deep esteem and sincere affection. I am therefore particularly glad to be with you, her spiritual daughters and sons. I especially greet Sr Nirmala, recalling the day on which Mother Teresa came to Rome to introduce her to me in person. I extend my thoughts to all the members of the great spiritual family of this new Blessed.

2. A "*Missionary of Charity*: this is what Mother Teresa was in name and in fact". Today with deep feeling I repeat these words that I spoke the day after her death (*Angelus,* 7 September 1997; *L'Osservatore Romano English Edition,* 10 September, n. 1).

First and foremost a *missionary*: there is no doubt that the new Blessed was *one of the greatest missionaries of the 20th century*. The Lord made this simple woman who came from one of Europe's poorest regions a chosen instrument (cf. Acts 9: 15) to proclaim the Gospel to the entire world, not by preaching but by daily acts of love towards the poorest of the poor. A missionary with the most universal language: the language of love that knows no bounds or exclusion and has no preferences other than for the most forsaken.

A Missionary of Charity. A missionary of God who is love, who has a special preference for the least and the humble, who bends over the human being wounded in body and spirit and pours "the oil of consolation and the wine of hope" upon the wounds. God did this in the person of his Son made man, Jesus Christ, the Good Samaritan of humanity. He continues to do this in the Church, especially through the saints of charity in whose ranks Mother Teresa shines in a special way.

3. Where did Mother Teresa find the strength to place herself completely at the service of others? She found it in *prayer* and in *the silent contemplation of Jesus Christ, his Holy Face, his Sacred Heart*. She herself said as much: "The fruit of silence is prayer; the fruit of prayer is faith; the fruit of faith is love; the fruit of love is service; the fruit of service is peace". *Peace,* even at the side of the dying, even in nations at war, even in the face of attacks and hostile criticism. It was prayer that filled her heart with Christ's own peace and enabled her to radiate that peace to others.

4. A missionary of charity, a missionary of peace, a *missionary of life*. Mother Teresa was all these. She always spoke out in defence of human life, even when her message was unwelcome. Mother Teresa's whole existence was a *hymn to life.* Her daily encounters with death, leprosy, AIDS and every kind of human suffering made her a forceful witness to the Gospel of life. Her very smile was a "yes" to life, a joyful "yes", born of profound faith and love, a "yes" purified in the crucible of suffering. She renewed that "yes" each morning, in union with Mary, at the foot of Christ's Cross. The "thirst" of the crucified Jesus became Mother Teresa's own thirst and *the inspiration of her path of holiness*.

5. *Teresa of Calcutta was truly a Mother*. A mother to the poor and a mother to children. A mother to so many girls and young people who had her as their spiritual guide and shared in her mission. The Lord brought forth from a tiny seed, a great tree, laden with fruit (cf. Mt 13: 31-32). And precisely you, sons and daughters of Mother Teresa, are the most eloquent signs of this prophetic fruitfulness. *Keep her charism unaltered* and follow her example, and from Heaven she will not fail to sustain you in your daily journey.

However, today more than ever, Mother Teresa's message is an invitation addressed to us all. Her entire existence reminds us that *being Christian means being witnesses of charity.* This is what the new Blessed entrusts to us. Echoing her words, I urge each one to follow generously and courageously in the footsteps of this authentic disciple of Christ. *On the path of charity, Mother Teresa walks at your side.*

I cordially impart to you and to your loved ones my Apostolic Blessing.

Appendix-V

PRAYER

Mother Teresa advised,

> "Try to feel the need for prayer often during the day and take the trouble to pray. Prayer makes the heart large enough until it can contain God's gift of Himself. The following prayers we say every day from our prayerbook."

- Deliver me, O Jesus,
  From the desire of being loved,
  From the desire of being extolled,
  From the desire to being honored,
  From the desire of being praised,
  From the desire of being preferred,
  From the desire of being consulted,
  From the desire of being approved,
  From the desire of being popular,
  From the fear of being humiliated,
  From the fear of being despised,
  From the fear of suffering rebukes,

From the fear of being calumniated,
From the fear of being forgotten,
From the fear of being wronged,
From the fear of being ridiculed,
From the fear of being suspected.
Amen.

- Dear Jesus, help us to spread Your fragrance everywhere we go.
Flood our souls with Your spirit and life.
Penetrate and possess our whole being, so utterly,
That our lives may only be a radiance of Yours.
Shine through us, and be so in us,
That every soul we come in contact with may feel Your presence in our soul.
Let them look up and see no longer us, but only Jesus!
Stay with us, and then we shall begin to shine as You shine;
So to shine as to be a light to others.
The light O Jesus will be all from You, none of it will be ours;
It will be You, shining on others through us.
Let us thus praise You without preaching, not by words but by our example,
By the catching force, the sympathetic influence of what we do,
The evident fullness of the love our hearts bear to You.
Amen.

- Lord, make me an instrument of your peace:
where there is hatred let me sow love;
where there is injury, pardon;

where there is doubt, faith;
where there is despair, light;
where there is sadness, joy.
Lord, may I not so much seek to be consoled as to console;
to be understood as to understand;
to be loved as to love.
Because it is in giving that we receive,
in pardoning that we are pardoned. Amen.

- When I was hungry, you gave me food.
When I was thirsty you gave me drink.
Whatsoever you do to the least of my brethren, you do it to Me.
When I was a stranger, you opened your doors.
When I was naked, you gave me clothes.
When I was tired, you gave me peace.
When I was frightened, you calmed me down.
When I was lonely, you gave me your love.
When I was sick or wounded, you took care of me.
Looking for friendship, you gave me your hand.
When I was old, you smiled at me.
When I couldn't find peace, you brought it to me.
You were on my side in times of despair, and in the hour of joy, we were together. Amen

Mother Teresa's United Nations Prayer

(Mother Teresa composed this prayer for the United Nations International Year of the Family)

- "Heavenly Father, you have given us a model of life in the Holy Family of Nazareth. Help us, O loving Father to make our family another Nazareth where love, peace and joy reign. May it be deeply contemplative, intensely Eucharistic and vibrant with joy. Help us to stay together in joy and sorrow through family prayer. Teach us to see Jesus in the members of our family especially in their distressing disguise. May the Eucharistic Heart of Jesus make our hearts meek and humble like His and help us to carry out our family duties in a holy way. May we love one another as God loves each one of us more and more each day, and forgive each other's faults as You forgive our sins. Help us, O loving Father to take whatever You give and to give whatever You take with a big smile. Immaculate Heart of Mary, cause of our joy, pray for us. St. Joseph, pray for us. Holy Guardian Angels be always with us, guide and protect us. Amen."

- Mary, Mother of Jesus, give me your heart so beautiful, so pure, so immaculate,
  so full of love and humility that I may be able to receive Jesus in the Bread of Life,
  love Him as You loved Him, and serve Him as You served Him,
  in the distressing disguise of the poorest of the poor. Amen.

- Breathe in me, O Holy Spirit, that my thoughts may all be holy
  Act in me, O Holy Spirit, that my work too may be holy
  Draw my heart, O Holy Spirit, that I love but what is holy
  Strengthen me, O Holy Spirit, to defend all that is holy
  Guide me then, O Holy Spirit, that I always may be holy. Amen

- Remember, o most gracious Virgin Mary, that never was it known that anyone who fled to your protection, implored your help or sought your intercession was left unaided. Inspired with this confidence we fly to You, o virgin of the virgins, our Mother. To you we come, before you we stand sinful and sorrowful. O Mother of the word incarnate, despise not our petitions, but in your clemency, hear and answer us. Amen.

- Lead me from death to life,
  from lies to truth
  Lead me from despair to hope
  from fear to trust
  Lead me from hatred to love
  from war to peace
  Let peace fill our heart, our world
  our universe with peace. Amen

- Make us worthy, Lord, to serve our fellow men throughout the world, who live and die in poverty and hunger. Give them today, through our hands, their daily bread and through our understanding love, give peace and joy. Amen

- Hail Mary, full of grace, the Lord with with thee,
  Blessed art thou among women,
  and blessed is the Fruit of thy womb, Jesus.
  Holy Mary, mother of God,
  Pray for us sinners,
  Now and at the hour of our death. Amen

NOTES & REFERNCES

- *Mother Teresa*, by Navin Chawla, published by Penguin Books, New Delhi, in 2002
- *Reaching out in Love & Stories told by Mother Theresa,* compiled & edited by Edward Le Joly & Jaya Chaliha, published by Penguin Books, New Delhi, in 1998
- *Mother Teresa - A Simple Path,* compiled by Lucinda Vardey, published by Rider in 1995
- *Mother Teresa – Her People and Her Work,* by Desmond Doig, published by Nachiketa Publications, London, in 1976
- *Mother Teresa – Beyond the Image,* by Anne Sebba, published by
- *The Hindu – Frontline Magazine,*
- *Time Magazine – September 1997 Issue*
- *Website: www.worldofbiography.com*
- *Website: www.nobelprize.org*
- *Website: www.wikipedia.org*

- *Website: www.news.bbc.co.uk, 2002*
- *Website: www.cnn.com*
- *Website: www.time.com*
- *Website: www.rediff.com, 2003*
- *Website: www.india-today.com, 1997*
- *Website: www.usatoday.com September 1997*
- *Website: www.Chron.com, September 1997*
- *Website: www.washingtonpost.com, September 1997*
- *Webiste: www.laymc.bizland.com, September 1997*
- *Website: www.franciscan-sfo.org*
- *Website: www.kathrynspink.co.uk / talk.htm*
- The Houston Chronicle News Services, September 1997
- Associated Press, September 1997
- *Website: www.missionariesofcharity.org*
- *Website: www.vatican.org*
- *Website: www.rmaf.org.ph*